GERMAN NEW RIVER SETTLEMENT: VIRGINIA

By Rev. Ulysses S. A. Heavener

REPRINTED WITH A NEW INDEX
By Anita Comtois

CLEARFIELD

Originally Published
ca. 1929

Reprinted with a New Index
Genealogical Publishing Co., Inc.
Baltimore, 1976

Reprinted for
Clearfield Company, Inc. by
Genealogical Publishing Co., Inc.
Baltimore, Maryland
1992, 1994, 2002

Library of Congress Cataloging in Publication Data
Heavener, USA
  German New River settlement, Virginia.
  Reprint of the 1929 ed.
  Includes index.
  1. German Americans—New River Valley, Va. and W. Va. 2. New River Valley, Va. and W. Va.—History. 3. New River Valley, Va. and W. Va.—Genealogy. I. Title.
F232.N5H44 1976   975.5'7'00431   75-28471
ISBN 0-8063-0690-4

Copyright © 1976
Genealogical Publishing Co., Inc.
Baltimore, Maryland
All rights reserved

CONTENTS

The First Settlement Beyond the Alleghanies [3]

German Pioneers of New River Settlement 20

Civic and National Relations 28

Church Relations 31

Baptismal Lists 46

List of Earlier Marriages 54

Land Patents and Grants 57

Some Additional Family History 61

Index 77

CHAPTER ONE

"The First Settlement Beyond The Alleghanies"

The caption that furnishes the subject for the first chapter of this narration, as above, is not original with the writer, but has been used by other writers and historians as referring to "Draper Meadows" settlement, as well as to be used in reference to the whole settlement of southwest Virginia; but more especially the "Middle New River Settlements." The purpose of the writer is to give the subject a restricted sense. Not in the spirit of controversy or antagonism, but merely to arrive at conclusions, based upon indubitable facts the writer is put to the necessity of showing that the "German New River Settlement," centering in and around the "Horse shoe bottoms" of New River and the mouths of Thoms and Stroubles Creeks and extending from this center has priority claims over "Draper's Meadows" by several years.

New River that occupies such a large place in this narration, rises in the mountains of North Carolina and takes a northwesterly course across southwest Virginia. At the mouth of, and in conjunction with Gauley River, the name is changed to the Great Kana-wha River and flows into the Ohio River and so its waters finally reach the Gulf of Mexico. New River flows through a mountainous section for about the first third of its course in North Carolina and Virginia, the same being, also, true of the last one third through West Virginia. The middle third of this stream crosses the plateau of the great valley that extends from Pennsylvania to Chattanooga, Tennessee. In this region is to be found some of the most fertile land in Virginia. The river winds about forming big and little horseshoes here and there, and at many other points precipitous bluffs project out over the water making the valley of the river at many points scenes of beauty and picturesqueness, almost unequaled.

Why the river was called "New River" will, perhaps, never be definitely known. There are a number of conjectures. One is that when discovered by Wood and his party it was called "New River" because unknown to the Colonists. It however frequently bore the name of "Wood's" for a long while, even up to, and as late as 1770. Another conjecture is that it is an Indian name meaning "New Water." Hardesty in his Geographical History says, that Captain Byrd who had been employed in 1764 to open a road from James River to where the town of Abingdon now stands, probably using Jefferson's map of Virginia engraved in France in 1755, and on which this river did not appear, named it "New River." This conjecture is not valid for the reason that court records as early as 1745 in Orange Court House mention "New River" on that date. (See Road Orders in this chapter). If conjectures are in order, the writer suggests another one. It is fair to assume, and we believe it to be true, that the name Kanawha was the name of the entire river and was so named after a tribe of Indians which occupied the mountains of what is now Floyd and Carroll Counties by name of "Canawhay" (see Johnston on the Middle New River Settlements). Adding to the assumption that the whole river was more than likely called "Kanawha," yes may we say, more than an assumption when you locate the tribe of Indians in the upper middle New River. Now add to this fact the further fact that it was the universal habit among the Germans and others of our New Middle River Settlement and the region generally, to change and shorten all names of people and places and things. May it not be that it runs something like this:—"Kanawha was contracted to, and called for a while "Nawa" and "Nawa" was contracted quickly into "NEW." Still all are conjectures.

It is difficult to make a boundary of the first settlers of New River, for early, the river valley as an objective was soon filled up by the Germans from Sinking Creek clear to Reed Creek where the settlers were mostly Scotch and Irish with a few of the same scattered here and there between the two creek valleys. There are, however, incontrovertible reasons for affirming that the center and beginning of what Mr. Johnston calls the "Middle New River Settlements" was the famous "Horseshoe Bottoms" and the immediate contiguous bottoms. This Horse Shoe and its contiguous bottoms mean of course, the bottoms at the mouth of Thoms, Stroubles and Back creeks, and these were not only the center and beginning of the "Middle New River Settlements", but were for a period of time, a unit, and as such becomes the "German Settlement of New River". From this common center all movements and settlements were made, including all creeks and valleys between Sinking and Reed Creeks and especially extending up the valleys of Thoms and Stroubles Creeks and including the plateau between them. There is no record for settlers on Sinking Creek till 1749, while there were settlers on Reed Creek by 1745, and "Tunker's Bottoms" prior to 1745. Almost as soon as the settlers filled up the bottoms contiguous to the Horse-shoe, they settled next in order, the plateau, around the site of Old St. Michael's-St. Peter's Lutheran Church, which includes the surroundings of Price's Fork. Here settled the Germans which was called the "German New River Settlement" and regarded in the Virginia Historical Magazine by a Lutheran writer as being a "lost" settlement.

We regard, then, as the center of a large area of the New River settlements, the Horse-shoe Bottoms (Faust in his History of the German People in the United States claims that the New River

Settlement of Germans extended to Sinking Creek and the Swiss Settlement around Newburn the old County seat of the now Pulaski County) and the Lover's Leap, the geographical center of the more restricted German New River Settlement.

Tradition has it that "Lover's Leap" was so called because it was a trysting place for Indian lovers, and a disappointed or jilted lover leaped over the cliff to his death. This "Leap" is from a large cliff of some two hundred and fifty feet, a perpendicular line from the farthest out point, reaching almost to the water's edge as the base, and situated at the left hand toe of the Horse-shoe bend of the river as you face it. Much of the cliff has been blasted away in the construction of the Virginia Railway. This rock is frequently used by picnic parties and travelers go out of their way to see it. From this eminent vantage point, like Moses looking out from Mount Nebo, viewing the Promised Land o'er, you can see the whole of the land mostly encircled by the river, a fertile tract of land ranging in acreage from two to three thousand acres; the Wall bottoms at your left where were located the Walls and just a little farther up the mouth of Stroubles Creek where the Shells first located, while the majestic river may be seen for miles as it flows on untiring in its course. The scene here is most beautiful and fascinating and is held by many to exceed the view of the French Broad. Some two and a quarter miles down the river Thoms Creek empties into the river while about three quarters below this is the "Adam Harman Ford" the first outlet to the whole southwest Virginia and Kentucky and in 1745 the official terminus of the "Indian Road" the first to be ordered by a court to extend from the Frederick County Line. To your right can be seen a little of the Buchanan Bottoms, but first the home of Adam Harman, next adjoining thereto were located the Harless and Michael Price bottoms. To your rear, lies the lands adjacent to Price's Fork, getting its name from the Price's who first located here and from the divide in the roads leading to Adam Harman's Ford and Pepper's Ferry. This fork gives rise to a community center and rendezvous, the first beyond the Alleghanies. This Horse-shoe Settlement, the stopping point and gateway of all the early expeditioners, including Colonel Walker and his party, the Lincolns, Taylors and others who went to Tennessee and to join Daniel Boone and others in Kentucky, and such was known to Daniel Boone himself.

Augusta and Frederick Counties were formed at the same time and were to include the whole Valley of Virginia and all territory west of them. Augusta, the larger of the two, included a part of the now Bath County and all the southern and southwestern part of the Valley of Virginia, and the whole of southwest Virginia, West Virginia, Kentucky, Ohio, Indiana, Illinois, Michigan and Wisconsin. The size of the county and the distance the people had to go to court, the county seat being Staunton, first mentioned in the records as a town, 1748, caused early an agitation for the division of the county. These County Courts were important to the early settlers, as they represented practically the whole function of government; judicial, executive and legislative. The wishes of the people were complied with and accordingly the county of Botetourt was formed in 1770, with Fincastle as the County Seat.

The lines of the original county of Botetourt need not be given. It however, contained a part of the present Giles County and.Thoms Creek of Montgomery County is mentioned in the wills of 1772 as being in that county.

In 1772, Fincastle County was formed with Fort Chiswell now in Wythe County as the county seat, and near to, or at the Lead Mines and not on the State road leading to Bristol as would seem to be indicated by a monument on said pike. Fincastle County did not function but four years when the State Legislature of 1776 made its territory into three counties, Montgomery, named for James Montgomery, famous Revolutionary soldier, Washington and Kentucky. Washington County has since been sub-divided into numerous other counties in southwest Virginia, while Kentucky later passed into the State of Kentucky. The records of Fincastle County are at Christiansburg Court House. The lines of Montgomery were later shifted and its territory contracted by the formation of numerous other counties in the now State of West Virginia. The counties, then as related to the German New River Settlement, nominal and actual were in order of time as follows:— Essex, Spottsylvania 1720, Orange 1735, Augusta 1738, Botetourt 1770, Fincastle 1772, Montgomery 1776, Giles 1806 and Pulaski 1839.

The first white people to settle in the Valley of Virginia was the German Settlement as conducted by Adam Miller (Muller) at Massanutten in 1726. Joist Hite (Heydt) and other Germans settled in the lower Shenandoah near Winchester in 1732 and a little later another settlement of Germans was made at Peaked Mountain, not far from the town of Elkton on the Shenandoah River. From 1730 to about 1750 there was an inrush of German, Scotch and Irish immigrants into the Valley of Virginia, the latter of whom located pretty well over the whole Valley of Virginia while the Germans were inclined to locate in well-defined settlements.

We come now, more directly to the proposition with which we are concerned, *when and what* was the "First Settlement Beyond the Alleghanies" and where was its exact location? Any numbers of histories, all deriving their information, evidently from a common source, state that "Draper's Meadows" is the place and has priority in point of time. "Draper's Meadows" was later purchased by William Preston which he named "Smithfield" in honor of his wife. The College Farm of the Virginia Polytechnic Institute includes a part of this tract. In Dr. Hales' History of Southwest Virginia the following statement is found: "Thomas Ingles, a widower from Ireland, with three sons, Matthew, William and John, settled first in Pennsylvania. According to tradition, Thomas Ingles, in 1774, accompanied by his son Wililam, then a youth, made an excursion into southwest Virginia, going as far as New River ,and is supposed to have formed the acquaintance of Colonel James Patton, who then, or soon thereafter, held a grant of one hundred and twenty thousand acres of land. About the year 1748, the Ingles, Drapers, Adam Harman, Henry Leonard and James Burk, removed from James River and settled at Blacksburg." See also Waddell's History of Augusta County.

At this juncture we wish to make some notations concerning the above quotation. James Patton never lived in the precincts of New River. He lived near to, and was a member of the Tinkling Spring Presbyterian Church near Staunton. His Land Patent so called of one hundred and twenty thousand acres of land evidently covered broadly all his land patents, and so covering much of the land of "The Middle New River Settlements" and concerning which, he and his executors had well nigh endless litigation, for the reason that the Patent covered, like a blanket, much land that had already, and some years before, been entered and improved by others, and involving our German Settlers of New River. The writer counted more than one hundred Land Patents of James Patton, but has *never* as yet found the one for the "one hundred and twenty thousand acres." This is significant. It is however, true that he was killed by the Indians not at Draper's in the year 1756, as has been reported—but at North River 1755. (See Preston Papers.)

Adam Harman never lived at Draper's, nor on the James River, as we shall see in his first land claim. His home was at, and below the mouth of Thoms Creek. About 1746 he evidently was located about the McDonald farm just above Price's Fork, as this land belonged to his brother Jacob, or perhaps to both Jacob and Adam, as Adam was to "oversee and build the road from his home to New River" where he still claimed land. At the time of the rescue of Mrs. Ingle from her captivity by the Indians, he lived at least part of the time at Eggleston, now Giles County. He moved to Eggleston and Sinking Creek in 1749. This change of residence and the renunciation of his land and home below the mouth of Thoms Creek, for the wilds of the mountains of Sinking Creek region can be easily accounted for when we recall his great hunting proclivities.

In controversion of the above historical quotation and the claims of all other historians that the "first settlement beyond the Alleghanies" was Draper's Meadows" we wish to present documentary facts and other considerations to support our claim that the "German Settlement of New River" has priority claims by several years.

I. *Big Hunting and Fishing.* We shall present, first in order, high probabilities in the case. This is justifiable for the reason, as one philosopher puts it, probability is, after all one of the chief guides of life. One of these probabilities has to do with the fertility of the soil of the land in question. Some years ago Judge Simmons of Fincastle, in writing to A. B. Fauste, as above referred to, said: "The German people always *sought* the best land and always paid for it." So in this case, the real objective would be the richest, most fertile land available. Where will one find richer, more productive soil for crops and bluegrass, so essential for deer and elks in their wild state of life, than you can find in the bottoms of the famous Horse-shoe and the adjacent bottoms at the mouths of Thomas and Stroubles Creeks? Too, much of these bottoms was thickly covered with large oak trees which contributed to habits of wild game. It would now require a cash offer, of from two to four hundred dollars per acre, for much of the land before such offer would hardly be considered. Consider, too, the most excellent mill sites scattered here and there on these two creeks, so essential in the building of communities in a formative period. That the Germans showed a decided preference for limestone soil, is abundantly supported by the history of other settlements.

Consider, too, the fishing and hunting possibilities of this section, as against other communities, in the whole section of the Virginia southwest, so essential, thus making living possible in a pioneer period and easier under favorable times and conditions. That, hunting and fishing were real objectives is made clear in all the earlier Land Patents. The first such on record for the Horse-shoe as obtained by Jacob Harman 1752, and the one of same date for Adam Harman for the land below the mouth of Thoms Creek and those for Philip Harless, and all others, state that the purposes were for *"fishing, hunting, hawking, fording* and *all other benefits."* Here follows an interesting record from Staunton Court Archives: "On the eighteenth day of May, 1750, William Harbison, a Justice of the Peace for Augusta County, certified before the court that about the last of April, 1749, a party of seven Indians robbed the house of Adam Harman on New River of nine deer skins, one elk skin; that on the next day six Indians robbed the same house of fourteen deer skin and one elk skin; and the next day several Indians came and took away seventy-three deer skins and six elk skins." Now here is a total of ninety-six deer skins and eight elk skins. Who can say other than that Adam Harman was a great hunter? Incidentally, wild animal skins were the legal tender of the settlement, and perhaps so for a number of years. But why so many deer and elks? Because of the natural bluegrass producing bottoms of New River, particularly of the parts under consideration.

Colonel Walker, with five companions, made an expedition through southwest Virginia, extending into Tennessee and Kentucky in 1744. In Theodore Roosevelt's "Winning of the West" Vol. I, p. 174, and in a foot note you will find an interesting account of this expedition. It is as follows: "Walker and companions were absent for six months. He found traces of earlier wanderers, probably hunters. One of his companions was bitten by a bear; three of the dogs were wounded by bears, and one killed by an elk; the horses were frequently bitten by rattlesnakes; once a bull buffalo threatened the whole party. They killed *thirteen buffaloes, eight elks, fifty-three bears, twenty deer, one hundred and fifty turkeys and some other game.*" (Italics ours.)

Now the foregoing deposition and citation reveal what is here contended for, that, in the region of which New River German Settlement was the rendezvous and a geographical center, was exceedingly full of all kinds of wild game. This was due, perhaps, to the fact that it was neutral ground between the Indians of the North, none being nearer than the Cherokee tribes in the vicinity of Winchester of the lower Shenandoah River and the Kanawai tribe of Little River and vicinity, and others of farther South and southwest.

II. *A Missionary Trip.* We next come to the consideration of some very interesting history touching our community life.

Albert Bernhardt Fauste, in his History of the German People in the United States, Vol. 1, pp 206-208 says: "There remains to be noticed a few settlements in the extreme west of the Colony of Virginia, established before the Revolutionary War, at the outposts of civilization. Two of them were located on Patterson's Creek and the South Branch of the Potomac River, and the third settlement was on New River." The first two of these settlements are in West Virginia, not far from the city of Cumberland, Maryland, both being located in fertile valleys. Even these two settlements were regarded as "remote from civilization." The third settlement on New River, was about two hundred and fifty miles to the south, southwest. Fauste refers to visits to these settlements by Moravian Missionaries by names of Schnell, Gottschalk and Spangenberg. In the Archives of the Moravians, locked up in their vaults in Bethlehem, Pennsylvania, are descriptions of some of their visits to the above settlements. One of these trips is quoted, as described, in the Virginia Historical Magazine and Biography Vol XI and XII, is reserved for the chapter on Church Relations.

In 1749 Schnell and one other Missionary named Brandenmueller, (the citation in the Virginia Magazine, as just mentioned, seemed to indicate that Schnell made this trip alone) left their home and kindred, and started on their long and perilous journey on foot. They passed Frederick and Hagerstown, Maryland, thence up the Potomac River to Warm Springs, (now Berkley Springs, West Virginia) thence up the Potomac Valley, to the South Branch of the Potomac, to the first settlement on said South Branch, and thence on over to that of Patterson's Creek. Then retracing their steps to the first settlement named, thence up the South Branch of the Potomac for some distance, then across stretches of country without seeing a single white human being, or no human person at all, to the Greenbriar River, thence across the Shenandoah Valley to the German settlers of the Massanutten Mountain and those of the Peaked Mountain, then on to the James River which they swam (and that in November), and on, till they arrived at an Irishman's hut near Fincastle of Botetourt County. Here they staid all night sleeping on bear skins before the open fireplace, where slept the whole family. They had nothing to eat, but bear and deer meat and "Johnnie cake", being deprived of even cheese, as was stated. From this humble hut, they started the last lap of their journey of thirty miles to Jacob Harman's, who then lived in the Horse-shoe bottoms of New River.

Now this missionary trip of 1749, indicates that the settlements, and so of that of New River were made some time prior to that date. It is significant, that "Draper's Meadows" is not mentioned, at all, in this diary. Consider, too, that Bethlehem, Pennsylvania, was a long way off, when you consider the condition of the roads as had been made and the primitive methods of travel. Time was required to make a settlement, and time required to convey information, that such was formed, and, as usual, time elapsed while such projects were considered before volunteers could be had for such perilous undertaking.

III. *The First Law Suit.* The following indenture in the old Augusta records, involving land in the German New River Settlement is of interest and value in this connection:

Michael and Augustine Prive versus Lorton and Patton. In July 1748, the Price's agreed with Israel Lorton to purchase from Lorton, land on New River. Lorton bought three tracts of land from James Patton. The first contained four hundred acres at the mouth of Jones (Thoms) Creek, where Lorton had *entered* and *improved*, called Lorton's first improvement. Second four hundred acres at the Horse-shoe bottoms, called Lorton's second improvement. Third four hundred acres at Beaver's Dam, called Lorton's third improvement. The Prices bought first and second. Bill filed 1751. Tract number One is in the possession of Philip Harless and Michael Price. Tract number Two is in the possession of Augustine Price and his brothers, Daniel and Henry.''

The historicity of the above quotation cannot be questioned. It reveals several things. Thoms Creek was first called Jones Creek. Why its name was changed and why it was called Thoms Creek, will, perhaps, never be known. Tract number One was not *at* the mouth of Jones Creek, only in a general way, as speaking of and writing at Staunton. Philip Harless in his own right, took out a Patent for land lying ''between Adam Harman's Patent and old man Lorton's''. Now this Lorton farm of four hundred acres is the farm next above the land of Philip Harless I. and now known as the Keister and Gilmore farms, for which Harless and Price (Michael) took out a Joint Patent 1754 and corrected 1765, a part thereof, of which was later deeded to Michael Price in 1769. The second tract, in the Horse-shoe bottoms and with all, or parts of the said land, changed hands a number of times, by giving and taking the surveys or ''squatter's rights'', the *first* Patent for the same, being given to Jacob Harman 1752, and who lived in the Horse-shoe, as we shall later see, in 1749. Evidently the Price brothers sold, almost immediately, their rights to Jacob Harman. In all the discussion of original ownership of lands anywhere in the Valley of Virginia, and so of the New River settlement in particular was, and must be determined, by taking up the land and so having what was generally known in legal terms, as ''Squatters' rights''. It is well to remember, too, that titles were vested in survey papers. Here is also a definite and original legal contest involving Patton with his blanket grants of one hundred and twenty thousand acres of land, much of which may have been only a claim, from the Colonial Governor of Virginia in the name of the King of England, James Patton, holding blanket Land Patents seems not to respect the rights of the early and sturdy Germans, a strange people who had settled upon, and claimed the lands. And since ''Squatter rights'' had become questioned, hence the *immediate* and *general* trend to Richmond for Land Patents, so as to secure the rights of the people, as first settlers. But what we are after, now, is not rightful ownership, but priority of residence, which is here legally established some time before 1748 by Lorton, and Lorton is clearly not the first, or he would have taken the lands at, and around the mouth of either Thoms or Stroubles Creek before taking lands much less desirable.

III. *Court Orders for the opening and construction of roads.*

At the November, 1746, term of court for Augusta County, there were orders for three roads. They are not here given in chronological order, but in the order of climax as related to the

New River Settlement. One was to extend from Reed Creek in eastern Wythe County to a "ridge dividing the waters of New River from the waters of the South Branch of the Roanoke River." This ridge is but a few miles east or southeast of Christiansburg. James Calhoun and Charles Hart were named as overseers and the following workers were named: "George, Ezekiel and Patrick Calhoun, Bryant White, William Laidlow, Peter Rentfre and two sons, George the Tinker, Jacob Weelman and two sons, John Black, Simeon Hart, Michael Claim, John Stroud, Samuel Starnecker and all the Dunkers who were able to work on the same, and all other persons who lived in the precincts." The Dunkers lived on what was called "Dunker's Bottoms" near Radford. Let the reader notice the general absence of German names and the preponderance of Irish and Scotch names.

A second road was to extend up the Catawba Creek valley, from the James Rivers to the "waters of the North Branch of the Roanoke River". This order, of course supercedes the Orange County order of 1745, hereafter to be reported, and all other road orders going the same direction. Tobias Bright was named as overseer while William English and two sons; Thomas English and son; Jacob Brown, George Bright, Benjamin Oyle, Paul Garrison, Elisha Isaac, John Donahu, Philip Smith, Matthew English and the "rest of the settlers" were to be workers. Notice, again the absence of German names.

The third road, climatic in interest in this discussion, was to extend from the "waters of the North Fork of the Roanoke River to Adam Harman's, and from Adam Harman's to New River." Adam Harman was named as overseer, and the following were named as workers: George Draper, Israel Lorton and son, Thomas Looney, Jacob Harman and three sons, George Harman, Jacob Castle, John Lane, Valentine Harman, Adam Meser, Humbertson Lyon, James Shaggs (perhaps Schaggs), Humphrey Baker, John Davis, Frederick and two sons and "all other persons settling in the precincts." It will be seen that most of these names are German, while the Germans living in the extreme western portion of the road are not given, such as Jacob Scholl, Michael Preisch, Philip Horlas and perhaps others; but these must come in under the "all other persons that live in the precincts." Too, this list places George Draper somewhere between Blacksburg and Prices Fork in the year 1746, *two years previous* to the date for the founding of Draper's Meadows."

The fourth order, places a connecting link on the Catawba. It started on the "ridge above Tobias Bright's (named above as an overseer) that parts the waters of New River (meaning, of course, Thoms Creek) from the branches of Roanoke River, and leading to the lower ford of the Catawba Creek."

GERMAN NEW RIVER SETTLEMENT 13

Now the above four orders for roads give a continuous road from the James River to New River at Adam Harman's Ford. These all supercede the Orange County order for 1745.

For the sake of the history of the early roads of Montgomery County and to keep it together, we submit, of a later date, an order for road extending down the New River. I quote, as of date 1785 from the records at Christiansburg:—"Thomas Shannon and George Pearis (for whom Pearisburg is named) were appointed to view a road down the New River on both sides to the Greenbriar County Line."

We present, next in order, the road order of 1745 on record at Orange, County seat of Orange County, dug out by the writer and for the first time, so far as he knows, published. This eclipses, therefore, all other and later orders, as above. It presents the famous Indian Road up the Valley of Virginia, giving its beginning and terminus. It will be found in the records May Court of said county, 1745, and runs as follows:—

"On the thirteenth day of March, 1745, we, the undersigned subscribers, have viewed and laid off and marked the road in the said order as followeth, viz:— To begin at Thoms Brook and Frederick County Line and to go thence to Benjamin Allen's Ford and Robert Callwell's Path, and that Henry Fulkinburg, James Dalton, Charles Buck and Abraham Strickler be overseers of that part, and that they have for their gang all the inhabitants between the mountains from Frederick County line to Callwell's path; and that the road continue from Callwell's Path across Beard's Ford on the North River to Alexander Thompson's Ford on the Middle River, and that John Harrison, Captain Daniel Harrison, Robert Cream, Samuel Stuart, William Thompson and John Stevents be overseers and the same to have as their gang, all the inhabitants between the mountains between Callwell's Path and to Thompson's Ford; and that the road continue from Thompson's Ford to Tinkling Springs, and that James Carthy and James Carr be overseers, and all the inhabitants between the mountains above Thompson's Ford to Tinkling Springs, do *clear* the same; and that the road continue from Tinkling Springs to Beverly Manor Line and that Patison Campbell, John Buchanan and William Stevenson be the overseers, and all the inhabitants above Tinkling Springs and Beverly Manor do *clear* the same; and that the road continue from Beverly Manor Line to Gill Campbell's Ford on the North Branch of the James River, and that Captain Benjamin Borden, Captain William Evins and Captain Joseph Culson be overseers, and the gang to *clear* the same, be all the inhabitants above Beverly Manor Line and Gilbert Campbell's Ford; and the road continue from Gilbert Campbell's Ford to a Cherry Tree bottom on James River, and that Richard Wood, Gilbert Campbell, Joseph Sapsley and

Joseph Long be overseers, and that all the inhabitants between said rivers *clear* the same; and that the road continue from the said Cherry Tree bottom to Adam Harman's on the New, or Wood's River, and that Captain George Robinson, James Campbell, Mark Evins and James Davinson be overseers, and that all the inhabitants between the James and Wood's River *clear* the same." The Subscribers were James Patton and John Buchannan. (Italics ours.)

Now, as throwing further light upon the above road order, as to the terminus, location and direction of the famous Indian Road that led up the Valley of Virginia, and as to what part of Montgomery County the same passed through, and which practically furnishes the western boundary of the settlements we submit as a climax another, and the final road order.

In 1749 there was a court order from the court at Staunton the county seat of Old Augusta County as follows:— *"That all overseers of the Indian Road leading from Frederick County Line to Thoms Creek be retained till markers could be placed"*. (Italics ours.) These markers were to be a blaze and two crosses, as per order at Orange Court House of the 1745 road order.

The writer does not know all the particulars of the route of the famous Indian Road from its beginning to the James River, but certainly it is clear and undisputable that that road went from the James River up the Catawba Creek Valley, and if not by Draper's Meadow or Blacksburg, then, by the Barger Fort near the Ribble's and on, through direct to Prices Fork, passing evidently the Fort and Tannery at the McDonald farm and on down the New River ridge by Lover's Leap to, and below the mouth of Thoms Creek. In further proof thereof let us call your attention to two Land Patents. That of Jacob Harman as of date, 1752, cites the beginning of the whole Horse-shoe tract, said in the Patent to contain eight hundred and ninety-five acres, which is a mistake clearly or miscalculation, as to the number of acres, but says it was to begin at certain *"oak* and *ironwood trees"* at the *"Adam Herman Ford."* Where was this ford? Of the same date as the Jacob Harman Patent, as referred to above, one was taken out for Adam Harman for five hundred acres, the same to begin at the mouth of Thoms Creek, thence to run a northwesterly course and so as to circumvent the five hundred acres, coming to New River at a branch, then up the river to the beginning. Here, then, are evidences from the Land Office in Richmond, Virginia, and from Court Records at Staunton that are as definite as the English alphabet. Jacob Harman lived in the Horse-shoe in Dec. 1749 (see chapter on Church Relations) Adam Harman was interested in having the road extend to his place "on New River", the Orange Court Record says the road was to extend to "Adam Harman's on New River." Now this ford was about a mile or less below the mouth of Thoms

Creek and the only place to ford the river, at that time. As before stated this ford was the outlet for all movements to the southwest until the Pepper's Ferry was opened 1750 by Samuel Pepper. The route of the road after it crossed New River at Adam Harman's Ford, the same being later tapped by the road from Pepper's Ferry, extended across Pulaski County northwest of New River station and across the N. & W. Railway east of Dublin, striking the old Rock Pike about three miles east of Newbourne. It is also significant that the only ford on the James River is *just above "Cherry Tree Bottoms"*, and so in both cases antedate ferries.

Let us keep in mind that the dates of the above Land Patents have nothing to do specifically with the date of the settlements of the men named. These Land Patents in vogue around seventeen and fifty were a measure to secure property rights that inherred in date of settling on the tracts of land named, or by purchase from others, taking and holding the survey as the guarantee of property rights. But the dates do place Adam Harman on New River, certainly two or three years before March 1745. As before stated, the order for the road in 1746 to be built from North Fork of the Roanoke River to New River, places Adam Harman at some intermediary point, which was evidently at Jacob Harman's, who owned land at the McDonald farm adjoining land of Bane and Lorton at Beaver Dam on Thoms Creek. Jacob Harman Sr. was killed at North River by the Indians in 1756. His son Jacob fell heir to the farm just named and it was Jacob Jr. who deeded the farm to Byron McDonald 1768.

In an interview, by the writer, with Dr. Holmes, a respected and elderly physician in Pulaski City, and who was familiar with the first settlements of lower Thoms Creek, said the Prices, Harlesses had settled there as early as 1743. This interview was had in the summer of 1926. The Orange Road order will certainly place Adam Harman and others at mouth of Thoms Creek 1743, or earlier.

IV. *An Early Contiguous Settlement.* In Volume eleven of the Virginia Historical Magazine and Biography will be found the following historical statement: "The German Sabbatarians Ephrata Society, a part of which left Pennsylvania September 14th, 1745, and went about four hundred miles toward the setting sun, beyond all Christian governments and reached a stream which runs toward the Mississippi. Here they settled in the midst of a pack of nothing but ragamuffins, the dregs of human society, who spent their time in murdering wild beasts." The expression "murdering wild beasts" indicates that the quotation as above from the Virginia Historical Magazine has its origin in the write-up by the Sabbatarian Church itself, and brings to the fore the adventures of their own people. Of course its historicity is unquestioned.

This settlement, as before stated, was on the bottoms above Radford a little way. This settlement was effected, as you see, at the close of the year 1745. It found in the same vicinity the community of "Ragamuffins." Schnell, in his visit to the Horseshoe in 1749, refers to the Sabbatarians at the Dunker Bottoms. The moral or spiritual condition of the Sabbatarians would seem that the raggamuffins had become assimilated with them. However, this movement ceased by 1750.

V. *Historian Quoted.* In David E. Johnston's History of the Middle New River Settlements, he contends, on page nine, that the claims for the Draper's Meadows as the first settlement beyond the Alleghanies, *"has been for many years disputed."* (Italics ours.) He mentions that John Toney and family from Buckingham County settled at the junction of East, with New River in 1780. He found there the decayed remains of a cabin, and that some land had been cleared around the same, and nearby, he found a grave with a stone at the head, on which was found the following inscription:—"Mary Porter was killed by the Indians 1742." Then, followed something with respect to Mr. Porter which the crumbling conditions of the stone made illegible.

This pioneer Porter formed no settlement, but he was a brave hunter. The only known gateway to this home of Porter was through the German New River Settlement. That he entered that way can hardly be questioned. That he passed on down the river to East River, carries on the face of it, that the best blue grass, and other sections for fishing and hunting, was generally taken up. At least, Porter would hardly pass such by, as that was first to be seen of New River, in the vicinity of the Horseshoe.

We quote from another historian as given in the "SEMICENTENNIAL HISTORY OF WEST VIRGINIA" by James Morton Callahan. In his chapter on "Evolution of Settlements" page sixteen, he speaks of the early German Settlement in the lower Shenandoah and near Winchester, mentioning among others Joist Hite who settled in the region mentioned in 1732 and mentioned his legal difficulties with Lord Fairfax who had a large land survey covering much of the territory of Virginia and later West Virginia. as drained by the waters of the Potomac. This dispute was such as to make land titles insecure, especially for German people. This led to the emigration of many of the German people to southwest Virginia. We quote:—"Several German immigrants, induced by insecurity of titles in the lower Shenandoah, crossed the Alleghenies, built cabins in the New, the Greenbriar and the Kanawa valleys." This lawsuit was in the year 1736. This sounds as though the Germans joined the caravan of German immigrants who were moving up the Shenandoah Valley toward New River about 1738 and 1740.

VI. *The Archives of Pennsylvania.* There is further and final evidence to strengthen the conclusions herein reached. The Archives of Pennsylvania deal with two things touching this whole matter. The first has to do with the landing of the immigrants from Germany. Series three, I think, furnishes these lists. These are quoted by Roupe in his "One Thousand Germans in the United States." Those that settled, as the first settlers in the New River region, landed in Philadelphia 1738 and 1740, and a few before these dates. In the second place, the Archives of Pennsylvania give all the land owners and all tax payers during the eighteenth Century in that state, and in all these lists the names of our immigrants who came to New River, do not appear, which mean, of course, that they did not settle in Pennsylvania *at all*, but their names do appear, and only here, in the land deeds and patents in connection with New River.

And the significant thing about the Land Patents, is that those of New River are among the very earliest of Augusta County, as onyone may see in the Land Office of Richmond. The bottoms of New River, next below those adjacent to the mouth of Thoms Creek and just a little below the lower extremity of the Adam Harman five hundred acre tract, you will find some very fertile land adjacent to the mouth of Back Creek but on opposite side of the river, for which Sifford took out a patent in 1746. This is about the earliest date for any patent in all the region of New River, and in fact, antedates most others of the said James Patton. Sifford was a German and the mouth of Back Creek lands rightly belong to our German New River Settlement.

VII. *The First Survey.* Miss Ella McDonald, now deceased, and who was one of the best historians touching the Revolutionary War and Church matters of Montgomery County gave the information to the writer that the "first survey of the Horse-shoe was made in the year of 1738"; that the first owner of the Horse-shoe was a Mr. Robinson who traded the same for a shot-gun. There are other traditions that the Horse-shoe was sold for a yoke of oxen, and at another time for a horse, saddle and bridle, etc. It is clear that there were a number of owners for all, or part of the same until it was finally owned by Jacob Harman. It is furthermore a striking thing that Burk who is mentioned as conveying at an early date, land to Jacob Shell at the mouth of Stroubles Creek, Israel Lorton and son, and the Robinson just named should have passed out of the community life of the immediate confines of the Horse-shoe, the center of what we are contending for, as the "First Settlement Beyond the Alleghanies." This is, nevertheless, the facts in the case; and while they are rightfully to be included as among the first settlers, yet they vacated in favor of the Germans who held the ground, at all odds, and whose progeny hold the same to this day. That the "Peaked Mountain" German Settlement, was closely related to the New River Settlement of Germans, can never be questioned. After Braddock's defeat Daniel, Henry and Augustine Price returned to Peaked Mountain neighborhood, and lived out their natural life there. That Martin Harless visited Peaked Mountain is clear, for in 1769 a daughter, baby, of his, appears in the baptismal record of the Peaked Mountain Church. One of the early Jacob Harmans lived and died in the vicinity of the church just named. He was evidently a first cousin to Adam, Valentine and Jacob Harman brothers of the New River Settlement. That the last three, as just named, with Michael Price, John Philip Harless, Jacob Shell, Sifford, and perhaps one or two others did not tarry long at Peaked Mountain, is clear, but pushed immediately, almost, to the rich lands of New River.

VIII. *The Kindly Feelings Between the Germans and Indians.* Should it be said, that the dangers incident to moving to such a remote section of the vast wilderness waste, was such as to preclude the probability and possibility of such a settlement, it may be said that our settlers imbibed the feeling in passing through Pennsylvania that William Penn having treated the Indians so kindly, that the Indians were disposed to live in peace with the Germans. Penn's attitude toward the Indians must have been known far and wide among them. It is significant that no record of massacres by the Indians are left among the earlier German settlements. The Indians who broke into the home of Adam Harman in 1749 seemed not to have molested the life of any of the family. There were no molestations until the killing of Valentine Harman and the massacre at Draper's Meadow in 1755. It ought to be said, in this connection, that the Indians were generally peaceable toward the earlier settlers of southwest Virginia until the French and Indian Wars, being incited to commit depredations upon all white settlers, who were, supposed by French to be English settlers and sympathizers. The kindly feeling of the Indians, then, toward the Germans, as allies of William Penn, was that, that removed fear from the minds of the very first German settlers of New River Settlement, and was an *incentive for them to pass beyond all settlements* in the Valley of Virginia, and to *push beyond the very outposts of civilization*, where under virgin conditions a new civilization might be evolved.

Summing up then our case, and running in reverse order chronologically, we claim an earlier period than 1748, the recognized historical date for the founding of Draper's Meadow Settlement, by hunting expeditions and hunting rights as expressed in the earlier Land Patents; the Price Brothers against Patton and Lorton lawsuit, pushes the date some two or three years back of the date of the purchase of the three tracts of land by the Prices from Lorton in 1748, each of which piece of land was in the confines of the German New River Settlement.

The road orders recited above place the date of the settlement some two or three years back of 1745, the date of the first one. This order gives the beginning of the famous Indian Road of the Valley of Virginia as beginning at the "Frederick County Line" and its terminus at "Thoms Creek," or more correctly speaking the Adam Harman Ford just below the mouth of Thoms Creek. It is significant too, that this road order makes the road to cross the James River at "Cherry Tree Bottoms." Here is the only ford of the James River within reach and its terminus at the Harman Ford of New River the only ford within reach on said river as above. This you see was before the date of the ferries so that these fords were vital to the pioneers and expeditioners. The "raggamuffins" found by the Ephrata Sabbatarian in 1745 must have located on New River, at least by 1744. These with the Porter family in 1742 would not have pushed on to less desirable sections if the more favorable sections had not been preempted. And too, there is every high probability that the Indian Trail led right up the Catawba to New River at "Lover's Leap" and right down the river ridge to the ford of New River subsequently called Adam Harman Ford. So that the first great sight stretching out before one's eyes would be the famous Horse-shoe Bottoms, the most coveted of all land prizes. That the Horse-shoe was first surveyed in 1738, as claimed by Miss Ella McDonald, elsewhere noted, and first owned as a whole by a Robinson, and since the deeds and sales made by James Patton involve the four hundred acre tract of the Horse-shoe, above noted; and one for four hundred acres at the farm next above the survey of Philip Harless I. and sold to Patton to Lorton and by Lorton to Harless and Michael Price I. and the four hundred acre tract at Beaver Dam and the eleven hundred and thirty acre tract sold to the Price brothers, Henry, Augustine and Daniel would indicate on the face of it that Patton never got hold of the more desirable bottoms of balance of the Horse-shoe nor those at the mouths of Thoms and Strouble's Creeks. This means that some of the land was already taken by "squatters rights". This further means that the Harless, Harman, Wall, Price and Shell tracts were held originally by them and much of it held by their issue to this day.

The dates of our German immigrants landing 1738 and 1740 and the entire absence of their names from the tax rolls of Pennsylvania and their first appearance in old Augusta's records would place the date of the New River Settlement to be 1740 and certainly not later than 1741. Every consideration as deduced from documentary evidence and reason, compel us to say by 1741, and confidently believing this to be correct, we affirm that the "German New River Settlement" was the *"First Settlement beyond the Alleghanies."*

CHAPTER TWO

German Pioneers of New River Settlement

We aim to show in this chapter that the German River Settlers of New River were real pioneers.

A pioneer is an adventurer, one who marks out the way. He is sometimes known as a trail blazer. He risks property, health, and sometimes even life itself in establishing the outposts of civilization. He often suffers untold hardships in his perilous undertakings. Abraham was a pioneer. To find pasturage for his flocks he and other Semites left the waterpools of the Arabian desert, pushing eastwardly toward the fertile valley of the Euphrates, thence up said valley and around north of, then into Palestine, where he was supposed to have an opportunity to build up, and maintain his monotheistic faith, and establish a nation of Godfearing people. He was a religious pioneer as well as for civil life and institutions. Paul was a religious pioneer, and the great apostle to the Gentile World. He was called to establish the Christian faith in the whole Western World. He was the trail blazer for the establishment of Western civilization; for wherever the Christian missionary goes, there soon follows a revolution of some sort, always working toward human freedom and man's well-being.

The pioneers of Southwest Virginia were of several distinct types. First we have the explorer type. Batts, Sailing and Daniel Boone were of this type. Then follows the hunter and Indian trader type. Men of this class knew of Woods, or New River before there were permanent settlements anywhere. The next type is the explorer, surveyor and land speculator. To this type belong James Patton, John Buchanan and others. Sometimes they were preceded by the "squatters" and sometimes they preceded all comers. Then we have the hunter, who sometimes was a quasi settler, and then the hunter who settled permanently. But there were but few of even this blended type among the German settlers. Adam Harman came near to being of the purely hunter type; and while he settled permanently and finally at Eggleston's Springs on Sinking Creek, he evidently spent nearly all his life in hunting wild game. Certainly the permanent settler stands at the head of all the types of pioneers.

Batts and his party in 1671 was probably the first to make the discovery of Woods or New River. This expedition was made under the auspices of Colonel Abraham Wood and the river they discovered was called by his party after Wood. The fact that the Batts party found the initials "M. A. N. I." on a tree near New River indicates that some white hunter had preceded them.

Spottswood made his famous trip to the Valley of Virginia in 1716. This expedition led to the Massanutten and Opequon settlements. However, the claim that Spottswood was the first to lay eyes upon the Valley of Virginia is now found to belong to another, as unearthed by Dr. Wayland of Harrisonburg, Virginia. This honor belongs to John Ledderer who anticipated Spottswood by forty seven years, the extreme point to which he went, being at or near Strasburg. He was commissioned by Sir William Berkley to make explorations of Virginia, 1670. In 1726, John Peter Sailing and one McKey penetrated the Valley as far as Roanoke, at some point near Salem. Here, Sailing was captured by the Cherokee Indians, and carried off as a captive. He was later redeemed and made his way back to his home at Williamsburg by a circuitous route through Canada. As a direct result of this trip, he later became a permanent settler at the fork of the James River. After Sailing's return many outposts were made in the Valley,—Lewis and John Preston settled at Staunton, Alexander at Lexington, James Patton and John Buchannan at Buchannan. Both the Scotch-Irish and the Germans vied with each other in establishing new homes in the wilderness.

Most all of the Germans of the New River Settlement were of the farmer type. Their first object was to obtain tracts of fertile land, mill sites and other advantages that go with a permanent settlement. The story of these Germans is not unlike that of the Pilgrim Fathers, who left England, and later Holland, because of civil oppression and religious prosecution, and crossed a dangerous sea to establish a new civilization on the bleak shore of New England. These New England people endured every kind of hardship and exposed themselves to the savage attack, in order that they might enjoy the blessings of religious freedom. Our New River settlers came for the self-same purposes. They were mostly if not all from the Palatinate Germany and had suffered the scourges of a long and bitter religious war; there was more or less friction between the followers of Luther and Calvin. Sometimes they were literally driven from their home and native land on account of their religion. Whole colonies of them fled into England and Ireland and later came over to this country. They came to establish homes where they could train their children according to the tenets of their own church, without any interference from the state. Adam, Jacob and Valentine Harman, Michael, Henry, Daniel and Augustine Price, John Philip Harless, Jacob Shell, Adam Wall, were among the very earliest of these German settlers. Just a little later, there were other settlers who came from Germany and still a little later these were augmented by some who came from North Carolina where a German settlement had been made on Haw River about 1745, by Germans who had gone thither from Pennsylvania, "crossing Maryland and Virginia in wagons." Among these who came to New River were John and William H. Trolinger and sisters, and Jacob Smith who first settled in Sinking Creek Valley, but subsequently removed to Thoms Creek. The Trolinger's and John Philip Hevner settled near Newbourn. This is what Faust calls the "Swiss Settlement," though Hevner was born in Germany and Adam Trolinger, the progenitor of those mentioned above was born "on the Rhine."

The names of all, or nearly all, the German Settlers of New River are given in Rupp's German Immigrants, and also may be found in the original forms in the Archives of Pennsylvania who arrived at the port of Philadelphia in the eighteenth century. Practically all, if not all, of our New River Settlement came from the Palatinate. Only those who reached the New River or located near to and such as may be in some way, related to them are given below. No attempt is made to give them in chronological order. Those who may be interested may consult further, Rupp's work, or the Archives of Pennsylvania, series II.

The ship, Winter Galley, landed in Philadelphia, September 5th, 1738 from Rotterdam, Holland, with the following names among others "from the Palatinate:" Philip Horlash (Horlas in list for oath of allegiance) age 22; Adam Wahl, age 21; Steve Lang, (Long) age 35; John Michael Prus, age 19; John Philip Sibolt and Adam Schaeffer. On September 9th, 1738, the ship, Glasgow, had such names as Gottfrie Zerwas (Surface), age 40, and Adam Halbert (Albert), age 35. On September 16th, landed Henrick Ellinger (Olinger), age 21; on September 20th, Adam Drolinger (Trolinger, as above) and on December 1738, Thomas Lang. January 10th, 1739 there landed John George Albert; August 27th, Philip Jacob and Peter Scholl, John Philip Surfas and Peter Schaeffer; September 3d, 1739, 1740, George Wilhelm. John Philip Hofner landed on the ship, Neptune, September 4th, 1752 (the paternal great great grandfather of the writer). On this same boat was George Wilhelm. One of the Jacob Herrman's came in ship, Good Will, September 11th, 1728; Adam Herrman (Harman) is said to have crossed over in 1725; the other Jacob Herrman came over September 28th, 1738, and with him, Richard and Elizabeth. Jacob Hoebach (Hoopaugh) September 17th, 1727; John Hoebach September 19th, 1738. Henry Wilhelm (Williams) settled in the lower Shenandoah Valley 1726 but must have emigrated to the New River Settlement, as three orphan children are mentioned in the court records as having been bound to Augustine Price 1757. There were Philip, George and Michael, sons of Henry Wilhelm. Others landed as follows: Christian Barger (Berger) and Christian Schmidt (Smith) 1738; Martin Wahl 1738; Jacob Hornberger (Hahnberger) 1732; Michael Kipp October 10th, 1749; John Henry Kipp 1732; Balzer Leibroch 1750; Frederick Koster (Keister) and

GERMAN NEW RIVER SETTLEMENT 23

Virginia Grace, September 24th, 1737. Peter Koster, with Robert and Olive, September 11th, 1738; Peter Clemintine and John Ohlinger, 1749.

The names of William Augustine, Henry and Daniel Pruss (Price) do not appear in any of the lists of names examined. As they are mentioned frequently with Philip Harless and Michael Price, and as Michael's age is given as nineteen years, and as court records show that they were younger than Michael, and as a church certificate of Elizabeth Harless Smith, elsewhere published, shows that Philip Harless I. married a daughter of Jonah Hendrick Preisch, and as this last named person did not come to America, it is therefore conclusive proof, that the five brothers named at the beginning of this paragraph, came over in the same vessel with Philip Harless and Michael Price, and was brother to the latter and brother-in-law to the former, and in common with many others, their names do not appear because they were minors, Michael being mentioned because he had reached manhood. All five of these Price boys evidently made their home at first with Philip Harless. Michael and Philip Harless bought jointly the farm of "Old man Lowerton's" next above Philip Harless' 1753, taking out a Patent for it 1754, while the first land mentioned as having been purchased by Daniel, Henry and Augustine was the four hundred acre tract from Israel Lorton, 1748, in the Horse-shoe and being just across the river from Harless.

There is no proof that all the German Immigrants as given above came direct to New River, yet many of them did, and others did either come or their sons did soon thereafter. It will be of interest to locate them. Philip Harless and the Prices first located at the mouth of Thoms Creek, the Prices later removing to vicinity of Price's Forks, while Daniel, Augustine and Henry removed to Shenandoah River, at the Peaked Mountain Settlement. Harless lived and died at lower Thoms Creek. Jacob Herrman first lived just above Price's Forks and then in 1749, lived in the Horseshoe, and was living there in 1762, when the estate of James Patton was settled. Adam Harman lived first perhaps with his brother near Price's Forks and then alternately at or below the mouth of Thoms Creek. The Wall brothers, Martin and Adam lived at Wall bottoms just below mouth of Stroubles Creek. Jacob Shell lived and died at mouth of Stroubles Creek. Sibolt, Bargers and Schaeffers lived on upper Thoms Creek. The Surfases, mentioned, lived in upper New River Settlement, or their sons came into the community a little later. The Olingers went into the valley at an early date and some of them moved early into the neighborhood of Price's Forks. The Alberts went early into Sinking Creek. The Wilhelms, afterwards changed to Williams, located on Thoms Creek and Sinking Creek, and like most of all of the rest of their settlers, part of their progeny are scattered over the south and southwest.

The Bargers and Schmidts located on upper Thoms Creek Valley. The Kipps located near Old St. Michael-Peters Lutheran Church. The Keisters located on middle and upper Thoms Creek. Peter Hornberger located in vicinity of Vicar's Switch. The Long's first located in the vicinity of the James River, later some of whom went over to New River vicinity. The Leibroch's located on Sinking Creek at Eggleston's, and was neighbor to Adam Harman who was there in 1749. Peter Scholl, one of the very first Magistrates of Augusta County, appointed thereto, 1745, later went to Kentucky and became linked up with the Boone's. This Peter and Jacob Shell of Strouble's Creek were evidently brothers, as they came from Germany on the same vessel. The Lucases located in Giles County and later in Montgomery. The Linkhouse's are still located in Montgomery County and came over early from Germany. The Hevner's and Trolinger's located near New Bourne, the old county seat of Pulaski county, on the outskirts of New River Settlement.

The Burkes, Leonards, Ingles, Drapers who lived in the Draper's Meadows Settlement were Scotch and Irish. It may be of interest to state in this connection that simultaneously with our German Immigration, there was carried on extensive Irish Immigration. James Patton was a great promoter and is said to have crossed the Atlantic Ocean twenty-five times, bringing the Irish Immigrants. Many of them were not able to pay their passage, even, but were brought by Patton and settled on his patented lands as "redemptionists." These were required to make stipulated payments, with interest, until the entire amount was discharged.

As set forth elsewhere Patton covered much of the section from Blacksburg westward, with large and numerous Land Patents, and thus covering what we are contending for, as the German New River Settlement. The only suit at law, touching any land with Patton, was the case in chapter first of the Prices, as against Lorton and Patton. Instead of any known settlement for land bought from Patton, supposedly, we find that Patton's estate made settlements with a number of the Germans of New River. This was true with Philip Harless, Michael Price, and Jacob Shell. John Buchannan, James Patton and John Preston came into the Valley of Virginia in 1742, but lived in the bounds of the now Rockbridge County. They were in no sense settlers of either New River or "Draper's Meadows." John Buchannan took the bottoms of New River from the mouth of Thoms Creek down, taking out a Land Patent for the same 1763, Adam Harman having forfeited his right to hold the same because of non-payment of the yearly stipend due the King of England. Buchannan was a relative of Preston and Patton. William Preston who afterward became the owner of the Draper's Meadow land, was a son of the above John Preston and was officially the first surveyor of Montgomery County. He was born in Ireland 1729, and died at the home of Michael Price I. about 1783. Israel Lorton, called in Philip Harlan's Land Patent "Old man Lowerton", as you see was an early settler. He died, 1753, and was perhaps the first person ever buried just above Shiloh Lutheran Church, at the David Harless graveyard.

Resuming somewhat, let us recall the background of these sturdy Germans who made this first settlement on New River. They were persecuted and virtually driven from their homes in the Palatinate, and they went out in search for liberty and in the pursuit of happiness. They crossed the Atlantic, not in steam palaces, such as ply the waters today, and for years past, but in sail vessels of the more or less primitive type. They passed from Philadelphia through Pennsylvania and Maryland, fording the Potomac above Harper's Ferry at the old "Packford" and went up the Shenandoah in wagons and on packhorses to their final destination. From the Potomac they made their way often exposed to wild beasts, Indians and robbers. Dr. John Craig, the first Presbyterian minister ever in the Valley of Virginia, states "The Immigrants were often murdered."

Let us turn now to these German Immigrants in their new environment, in their new homes. For the first season or two they scarcely have anything to eat except wild meats. Their fare consisted of deer and bear meat chiefly and "johnny cakes" and at times perhaps, parched corn. Their clothing perhaps, mostly made of wild skins. Their homes were huts built on the ground, the ground serving as the floor for some years. These were built by log forts for protection from the Indians. They labored day by day without sufficient tools. They were without furniture in their homes, except stools and tables made of split timbers with pegs as legs. They sleep before the open fireplace on bear skins. They have no schools for their children and no churches to keep the "home fires burning." They had many other hardships and privations unknown to us and beyond our recognition all too numerous to mention.

The reader is doubtless familiar with many of the actual depredations of the Indians around 1750, including the murder of Valentine and Jacob Harman brothers, the massacre at Draper's Meadows 1755, the attack on Vause Fort a little later, the killing of Balzer Librook's children and many others. In the Staunton Court records of 1800, Augustine Price, then about eighty years old, deposed that he had often been driven from his home on New River by the Indians. Talk about primitive conditions and hardships, here you have it in its crudest and severest forms. Call them what you may, I call them *pioneers of the real heroic type*. There is no greater hero than the common man whose deeds and exploits are unsung and unappreciated by the busy humanity of today or any day. These early settlers labored, suffered and deprived themselves of every convenience in order that their descendents might become a happy and free people. They lie in unmarked graves at the old Harless graveyard near Shiloh Church, at the Shell's near the mouth of Stroubles Creek, at Prices Fork, at the Wall home originally owned by Michael Price I., and at the Old St. Peter's Church site. We have entered into their inheritance and today we pause to do them homage and pay tribute to their memory.

A common lot of suffering always tends to increase the spirit of brotherhood. This is due to the interdependence of the members of a community especially in times of stress. Their cause and lot become a common one. This tends, too, to increase the social amenities and sports of the community. So the pioneer life is not, altogether a dark picture. All log rollings and brush burnings, all raising of log huts, houses and barns, all church services, all baptisms and even funerals were made great social gatherings. Foot races, horse races and horseback ridings generally were common sports of the day. Hunting big game was evidently a great sport. It was so fascinating to many, especially to the first and second generation of sons that they neglected their farms to the point of financial loss and, perhaps ruin.

Yet in spite of all this, our pioneers had a hard and difficult lot. This is revealed further in the fact that most of them died comparatively young, notwithstanding the fact that they were generally of sound physique, superinduced by hard labor and out of door life. The little piece of poetry by Edward Hartley Dewart appended herewith, is quite a fitting close of this pioneer chapter.

"Not on the gory field of fame
Their noble deeds were done;
Not in the sound of earth's acclaim
Their fadeless crowns were won.
Not from the palaces of kings,
Nor fortune's sunny clime,
Came the great souls, whose lifework flings
Luster o'er earth and time.
For truth with tireless zeal they sought;
In joyless paths they trod
Heedless of praise or blame they wrought,
And left the rest to God.
The lowliest sphere was not disclaimed;
Where love would soothe or save,
They went by fearless faith sustained,
Nor knew their deeds were brave.

No sculptured stone in stately temple
Proclaims their rugged lot;
Like Him who was their great example,
This vain world knew them not.
But though their names no poet wove
In deathless song or story,
Their record is inscribed above;
Their wreathes are crowns of glory.''

All hail, Heroes, one and all! Tho' late we sing your praises today!

Foot Note:—There is some confusion as to which Jacob Harman lived in the Horse-shoe, 1763. At the settlement of James Patent estate, a Jacob lived in Horseshoe, but this must have been Jacob, Jr.

CHAPTER THREE

Civic and National Relations

The German pioneers of the restricted area of the New River Settlement did not achieve any known renown in the earlier days of the settlement, either for the Colony or Nation, in its formative period. It is our purpose to show a valid reason for this seeming delinquency. It is partly accounted for by the remoteness of the settlement from the more fully and permanently settled conditions of the Valley of Virginia. This is shown by the first census of the United States in 1785 to 1790. If we remember correctly, not a member of the New River Settlement is named in that census, while the number in Montgomery County as a whole is relatively limited.

Recalling that there were no molestations of the whites by the Indians till the year 1749, and no other in contiguous neighborhoods till that of Draper's Meadows 1755, but from this date on depredations were more frequent and more general. So the men of the German New River Settlement, as well as others, had all they could do to keep the Indians in check, defending their homes and property. Sometimes the situation was most distressing and urgent. This was especially true from about 1760 to the Revolutionary War.

It is said that in all the Middle New River Settlements, including parts of the now Bland, Carrol, Grayson and the center of the now Montgomery Counties, as well as some adjacent territory of North Carolina, there were frequent uprisings of Tories. And there were a few of the Germans of the New River Settlement who were accused of Torianism, the records however show that this was rarely proven. Yet for these Germans there were extenuating circumstances. They had a religious background of Pietism that caused them to be opposed to war. They had a natural aversion to it. Having ventured far from the confines of civilization with the purpose to make treaties with the Indians, as did William Penn. But, all too suddenly, the Indians change their attitude and policies and become exceedingly menacing and dangerous. They were evidently excited to depredations by the French who were opposed to the ever advancing and expanding settlements of the English, and Protestants generally. With these backwoodsmen of southwest Virginia, it was not a question so much of the independence of the Colonial States, as it was to end a war that was often atrocious, and so an immediate problem to all of them, especially as the magnitude of the problem of the Continental armies was little understood by these remote valley settlers. This difficulty is greatly enhanced when we recall that our German forefathers conversed only in the German dialect. This is proven by the fact that the literature

GERMAN NEW RIVER SETTLEMENT

left by these people were German Bibles and Hymn books. Services were conducted in the German language in Old St. Peter's Church till about 1840. This fact alone unfitted our German people for leadership of any kind. The leaders of the community came, naturally, of the English speaking peoples. They were the conceded leaders in civic and national affairs by all Germans.

We desire to present, however, a couple of matters that concern Montgomery County as the successor of part of the old Fincastle County, and which will certainly reach, and include our German constituency of the New River Settlement. (See American Archives, Fourth series, Vol. 1. p 1166. Also—"Early Settlers of Tennessee.)

The Freemen of Fincastle County met in convention at the Lead Mines, the county seat January 20th 1775, better than a year before the famous date of signing the immortal Declaration of Independence, and a year before the dissolution of the county as such. These men in convention assembled, made a declaration in itself a real forerunner of the Declaration of Independence of the Colonies from British Sovereignty. This declaration of the men of Fincastle County was addressed to the Hon. Peyton Randolph, Patrick Henry Jr., Richard Bland, Benjamin Harrison and Edward Pendleton delegates of the Colony of Virginia to the Continental Congress held in Philadelphia. It recites, with other things, the following statement and which shows incidentally the real situation that confronted these backwoodsmen: "Had it not been for our remote situation, and the Indian War which we were lately engaged in, to chastise these cruel and savage people for the many murders and depredations committed against us, now happily terminated among us under the auspices of our present worthy Governor, His Excellency the Right Honorable Earl of Dunmore etc". Appreciation was shown for aid already received, loyalty for the Protestant Crown of the English Government was recited and further loyalty to said Government was pledged upon conditions of relief for the American Colonies, otherwise "if no pacific measures shall be proposed or adopted by Great Britain, and our enemies attempt to dragoon us out of these inestimable privileges which we are entitled to as subjects, and to reduce us to a state of slavery, we declare that we are deliberately determined never to surrender them to any power upon earth but at the expense of our lives."

The above declaration was prepared and presented to Backwoodsmen assembled by the following gentlemen:—Rev. Charles Cummings, Colonel William Preston, Colonel William Christian Captain Stephen Trigg, Major Arthur Campbell, Maker William Ingles, Captain Walter Crockett, Captain John Montgomery, Captain Jesse McGarack, Captain William Campbell, Captain Thomas Madison, Captain Evan Shelby and Lieutenant William Edmonston. Colonel William Christian was chairman and Mr. David Campbell clerk. Not a single German appears in the above list of men, not that they were not patriotic enough, but because they were disqualified by their language. But who would contend that the thrifty enterprising Germans were not present, and present in considerable numbers? Too, where did these committeemen get their military titles? Not in the Revolutionary War but from the County Courts, being appointed thereto as leaders against the marauding and stealthy Indians. The Augusta County records show that Adam Harman and Augustine Price received such commissions, too. It is unfortunate that the record of the men who were present at the above convention was not taken and preserved so as to be handed down to succeeding generations for their valorous spirit.

In the movements and battles of Cornwallis and Tarrelton about Greensborough, North Carolina, in the Revolutionary War, menaced the people of the Northern part of the Colony of North Carolina as well as those of the southern part of Virginia. In fact they were seriously threatened. General Green appealed to Governor Jefferson of Virginia for help, who in turn appealed to Preston Sevier, Shelby and Campbell. Accordingly, Colonel William Preston on February 10th, 1781 ordered the Montgomery County militia to assemble at the Lead Mines, and on the day appointed three hundred and fifty men assembled, pursuant to the order of their commander. Major Joseph Cloyd assembled the men of middle New River, which would include the men of Back Creek of now Pulaski County, Thoms and Stroubles Creeks. Also a company went from Wolf Creek under Captain Thomas Shannon and Lieutenant Alexander Marrs. The combined number of these men who answered the call of duty will never be known to historians or to their posterity. But they made themselves felt, fighting against the British near Guilford County Court House (Wentworth) according to reports. Colonel Tarrelton in reporting his southern campaign, page 241, says that "at the battle of Guilford Court House he held the right of the British army and that his troops were *badly hurt by backwoodsmen from Virginia.*" (Italics ours.)

Prior to the Civil War only a few of the Germans of New River owned slaves, consequently most of their descendants were opposed to the Confederacy, but on the other hand favored the Union Cause, as was the case in much of southwest Virginia and east Tennessee. But even here, as they were aligned on either side in the issues of the Civil War, they all accepted humble places and did their duty as they saw it while their grandsons fought side by side in the Great World War as of *One Nation and Indissoluble Forever!*

CHAPTER FOUR

Church Relations

ST. PETER'S EVANGELICAL LUTHERAN CHURCH.

First of all let us present a background to the beginnings of church matters in the German New River Settlement. Let us recall the religious wars of Germany and the persecutions of the Protestants at the hands of the Roman Catholic Church. This persecution was such as to cause not only immigration to the American Colonies, but to England and Ireland, many of whom came to America subsequently. This immigration occurred, roughly speaking, in the years from 1720 to 1770. Our immigrants, then came from intolerable conditions into the Valley of Virginia, and on to New River to build for themselves and their offspring Christian communities where they could worship and serve God according to their own volitions.

Going back into Augusta's records there are some sidelights on community psychology of the early settlements in the county, that are striking and interesting. It is not uncommon to find an entry like the following: "Indicted for swearing and using profane language"; so and so hailed into court for "not bringing up their children in a Christian-like manner", having in case orphans committed to them by the court. Some of these cases had reference to parties in the German New River Settlement. What a help to the moral and religious forces of a community, and the country, if today they could have the backing and help of the county and state courts, and that the law of the land required that all children should be "brought up in a Christian-like manner!"

The brotherhood and comradeship spirit of these Germans were most beautiful. Disputes between some of them were "settled out of court", while others held land jointly under squatters rights and later by land patents and grants.

According to Missionary Schnell's Diary, as reported in the Williams and Mary Magazine, there were three German Settlements in the Valley of Virginia. These were Massanutten, Cedar Creek and New River. However, there was one at "Peaked Mountain", evidently named for the peaked form at the end of the Massanutten Mountain, and where one only has to see this mountain in order to realize why so called, and is on the Shenandoah River near Elkton of Rockingham County. Here a union church was built in the seventeen and fifties by the Lutherans and German Reformed people. This church is mentioned in the will of one Jacob Harman in 1763, it receiving from him a legacy of land. The second Church on this site erected 1804 still stands and is in use.

It was from this place that the Prices and others went to New River. Here Martin, the eldest son of Philip Harless visited in 1769, as the church records show that a daughter of his was baptized. Here too, Augustine, Henry and Daniel Price returned after Braddock's defeat'' and lived out their natural life, and evidently their bodies lie in the burying ground in this old church. A partial list of the baptisms of this old church is given.

Perhaps in the mind of Missionary Schnell, the settlement referred to above, and that of Massanutten were the same. However, it is now held that the Massanutten Settlement is quite distinct, and lies about seven miles to the west of Luray, where the Lee Highway begins to ascend the Massanutten Mountain. Hebron Lutheran Church in Madison County is recognized as the oldest Lutheran Church in Virginia. The pastor, Rev. Klugg of this old church visited the Massanutten Settlement prior to 1747 and organized a Lutheran Church which did its work of redemption for years, and is succeeded by three congregations the offspring of this old Church. These are St. Peter's at Shenandoah, St. Paul's at Grove Hill and St. Luke's at Alma.

It is also highly probable that the Peaked Mountain Church, above referred to was founded by the pastor of Hebron Church, the Rev. Mr. Klugg, and perhaps about the same time as St. Peter's of New River Settlement.

In the visit of Missionary Schnell, in 1749, to the Massanutten Settlement, and from thence enroute to New River, he described the needs of religion as great and in numerous cases, infants and numerous children were brought to him for baptism which for various reasons he declined to do, chiefly because the Moravians at that time did not baptize infants, and in some cases because of the absence of the fathers on hunting expeditions. In one case a mother chided Mr. Schnell severely by saying in effect, "What, is not the Kingdom of God for our children?" The plea in the New River for baptisms was so urgent that he broke his rule and baptized several. It is likely that the pleas for baptisms in all the remote German Settlements were the cause of Mr. Schnell changing his mind on the subject of infant baptism, for in 1751 he became a Lutheran minister and was settled over two Lutheran congregations in Pennsylvania. (Va. His. and Magazine Vol. 12 and foot notes.)

As a matter of very great interest as well as background and religious beginnings we quote Schnell's Diary of 1749—as found in William and Mary Magazine of 1904:

"I had difficulty in finding my way to New River; met a wolf, frequently waded waters; (took whole journey on foot) had hard work swimming the James River; went up the Catawba twenty miles, no homes or houses; stopped at Justice Robinson's who owned a mill (and lived somewhere on the Catawba Creek and perhaps in the vicinity of the McDonald's Mill; and perhaps the original owner of that mill); crossed the Catawba Creek twenty times." On Sunday, November the 19th, "we were glad in anticipation of seeing the New River today and asked the Lamb (his name for Christ) for a favorable reception among the Germans. I arrived just before noon and crossed the river to Jake Herman's who with his wife received us with great joy and love. November 20th preached on "I am King" John 18:3. On the 21st. staid quietly at Jake Hermann's; 22nd. Cold; 23d. J. H. went with me to Jacob Goldman's, whose wife is sister to my father-in-law; 24th. went back to J. H.; J. H. told me his grandfather by birth was a Moravian, and had been driven from his country on account of his religion. Preached on the 26th. (Sunday) on "Ten Virgins." We were a few miles from Seventh Day Adventists ("Dunkers" Just above Radford), but we had enough description of them. Left 27th" retracing our steps for Pennsylvania via the Valley German Settlements."

As with the Pilgrims who settled on the bleak shores of New England, the Bible was a sacred and necessary book. That our German Settlers brought with them the Bible cannot be questioned. In the will of Jonah Michael Price of 1802 "the big German Bible" (a pretty good asset for a boy who landed at the age of nineteen) was bequeathed to his grandson, Ludwig (Louis) who lived and died at Mount Tabor near Blacksburg. Likewise there is a hymn book that fell into the hands of this Louis Price's wife, the daughter of Philip Harless II. and named Margaret, often called "Peggy." The following entry is to be found in this hymn book:— "Philip Harless, his hime book, August 8, 1802." This is a German Lutheran hymn book published by Marburg and Frankfurt by Heinrich Ludwig Brunner 1795. Is bound in wood with metal clasps and with Martin Luther's picture as frontispiece. This book is in the possession of Prof. J. J. Price, great, great, great, great grandson of J. Michael Price I. and Philip Harless I. etc.

The catholicity and tolerance of these earlier German Christians are further shown by the love and joy manifested in receiving the Moravian Missioners and the real Christian spirit was later shown in their attitude toward other Christian bodies or denominations that came into that section. Methodist and others had regular preaching appointments in old St. Peter's Church, and this, too, when it meant necessarily a division in the organized forces of the General Church and depleted funds in St. Peter's treasury. One certainly cannot call them narrow.

Such is the background and incidental facts and beginnings of the Christian community of the New River Settlement. The first sermon ever known to have been preached in that Settlement was by the Rev. Mr. Schnell, as above, was on Nov. 20th, 1749 and at the home of Jacob Harman in the Horse-shoe on "I am King." The second being by the same man in the same house on the parable of "The Ten Virgins." "Behold what God hath wrought!"

It has been said that "God's first temples were groves." In the case of New River it was groves and homes and perhaps the larger forts as well as school houses. A fort existed doubtless near the mouth of Thoms Creek, one at Shell's near the mouth of Stroubles Creek, the mound of which is clearly visible in the old Shell Home yard to this day; one such existed at the home of J. Michael Price I. now known as the Wall farm, about a mile and a half east of Prices Forks and just a little later, a large one existed at the Harman-McDonald farm. This is the farm sold by Jacob Harman Jr. to Byron McDonald 1768. At this place there was a tannery and equipment for the manufacture of powder, from which place powder was furnished for the Revolutionary War, being conveyed to its destination on horseback. This place, then was a community of some size for the day and so furnished the nucleus and a center for an organized church. Here, then evidently was the first location for the organized Old St. Peter's Lutheran Church and was the birth spot for Methodism "Beyond the Alleghanies." Here the Methodists first met in the home of McDonald and on this farm they held Camp Meetings till 1826.

We desire now to enter more fully into the formal discussion of the beginnings of St. Peter's Church. According to records, this Church was originally called St. Michael's, while at one time it was known as "Prices Church" and about seventy-five years ago as "The Old Brick Church." But hereafter in this narrative we shall call its last official name St. Peter's. As we have no records to show exactly when the Massanutten Church or that of Peaked Mountain Church was organized, we do have some definite data to offer as to when St. Peter's was organized, or at least when it was in existence as an organized body. And we rightly contend for the point that St. Peter's was the oldest of the Lutheran Churches west of New Market, and at least, the fourth and more likely the third for the whole of Virginia. Accordingly, we present here the deed of that Church.

COPY OF THE DEED OF OLD ST. PETER'S

This indenture made this fifth day of August, in the year of our Lord eighteen and six, between John Preston, Frances Preston, John Breckenridge and John Brown, Executors to the estate of William Preston, deceased, who was the Executor to the estate of James Patton deceased, of the one part, and John Wall and Michael Surface Elders of the Lutheran Calvinistic Church on Thoms Creek and their successors for and on behalf of the said Church of the second part.

Witnesseth

That the said Executors for and in consideration of a promise made unto said Church by James Patton in his life time and the sum of one dollar paid unto the Executors at or before the ensealing and delivery of these presents, and by virtue and power and authority given and granted unto them in, and by the last Will and Testament of the said James Patton, deceased having bargained and sold, and by these presents to bargain and sell unto the said John Wall and Michael Surface, Elders aforesaid, and to their successors for the benefit of said Lutheran and Calvinistic German Church, one certain tract or parcel of land containing four acres, be the same more or less, being a part of a larger tract of seven thousand acres granted unto the said James Patton by letters bearing date of ——175—, lying in Montgomery County on a branch of Stroubles Creek and bounded as follows: Beginning at a stake by the edge of a meadow on the South side of the German Church on Jacob Price's land, and with his line crossing the meadow North 26 poles to a black oak, three white oak saplings and a pine, East 25 poles to two white oaks and a black oak sapling, South 26 poles to between a locust and white oak, and 25 poles to the beginning. To have and hold the said tract or parcel of land and every part thereof, with all rights, members and appurtenances unto the said John Wall and Michael Surface and their successors forever, to and for the use of the said German Church.

And the said John Preston, Frances Preston, John Breckenridge and John Brown, as Executors aforesaid, of the parcel or tract of land as above described and bonded, with all premises and appurtenances before mentioned unto the said John Wall and Michael Surface, and their successors, for the use and benefit of the said German Church, free from all claim or claims upon them, the said John Preston, Frances Preston, John Breckenridge and John Brown Executors aforesaid, and from all and every person or persons whatsoever shall and will do warrant and forever defend by these presents. In witness whereof the said John Preston, Frances Preston, John Breckenridge and Johs Brown as Executors aforesaid, have hereunto set their hands and seals the day and year first above written.

Signed and delivered in the presence of John Preston Ex'r (Seal) At Montgomery County Court August, 1806.

This Deed and sale of John Preston, Frances Preston, John Breckenridge and John Brown Executors of William Preston deceased, who was the Executor of James Patton deceased, to John Wall and Michael Surface, Elders of the said Lutheran Calvinistic German Church of Thoms Creek and acknowledged in Court by said John Preston, and ordered to be recorded.

Teste, Charles Taylor, Clerk.

Concerning the above deed we desire to offer some considerations. James Patton was murdered by the Indians at North River 1755. As indicated in the deed the seven thousand acre Land Patent was secured somewhere between 1750 and 1755. In fact the hundred or more patents secured by James Patton were between those dates. But the significant thing is, that Mr. Patton made a *"promise"* to the Lutheran-Calvinistic German Church that was in *existence* before his death. This promise does not appear in Mr. Patton's Will on record at Staunton. But he must have made the "promise", and the church folks kept the matter alive till a deed was secured by the congregation from the Executors of the estate of William Preston who was the Executor of the Patton estate. The Calvinistic element referred to were the direct followers of John Calvin in Germany but otherwise known in this country as the German Reformed Church, later changed to the Reformed Church. I doubt if they were ever organized into a church body at any time. At the date of the deed the church was standing on the lot and had been built some years before, probably as early as 1780. It is doubtful if there were any deeds secured for church property prior to 1800. Mention is made in the will of Adam Wall 1799 (and Land Patent) of a schoolhouse that stood at one corner of his place near the mouth of Stroubles Creek. A schoolhouse stood close by the present Shiloh Church before the Civil War, and likely this was preceded by another, all of which were evidently used for places for public worship, as indicated above.

St. Peter's Church was evidently organized early at the McDonald Fort and moved to the site, as located in the above deed about 1770 and the log building that was standing 1806 was built about 1780. This site was chosen because it was central to the people of the upper Thoms and Stroubles Creeks, as well as to the lower sections of said Creeks, as well as the settlements that spread from each Creek, and centering at the site of the church.

The next definite document touching this old congregation is the Elizabeth Harless Smith Church Certificate, found in the effects of "Uncle Sammy Smith" as he was known for a long while by Prof. J. E. B. Smith, Principal of the Christiansburg High School and a great grandson of the party cited. The Certificate follows in full and which is of great historical interest in these narrations, bearing definitely upon a number of important facts. It was written in the German language and translated into English by Prof. A. G. Williams of William and Mary College. The certificate follows in full:

'In the year of grace after the victorious birth of our beloved Lord and Saviour Jesus Christ, 1768, the second day of July, there was born of virtuous wedlock, Elizabeth Harless. Her father John Philip Harless, a son of the deceased John Philip Harless, and his mother Anna Margretha, whose maiden name was Preisch. Her father was Hendrick Preisch and her mother Agnus.

The above mentioned Elizabeth's mother was Johannah, whose maiden name was Boscher. Her father was George Boscher, and her mother Elenora Charlatta. Her godfather and godmother were the deceased George Wilhelm and his wife Margretha.

According to the testimony of her above mentioned parents, Elizabeth was baptized in her childhood and was instructed by me in the doctrines of Christianity and thereupon was confirmed and pledged herself to lead a life of virtue and of piety, and thereupon was permitted, for the first time to receive the Lord's Supper and thus received and recognized as a member of the sacred Lutheran Congregation by me in open meeting.

Peter M. Brugell, D. D. W.,

Virginia, in Montgomery County on the first day of June 1788.''

The above letter reveals that Elizabeth Harless, who about 1790 married Jacob Smith, was born 1768, was the daughter of Philip Harless II. and that her sponsors were her uncle and aunt, George Wilhelm and his wife Margretha Harless Wilhelm, the daughter of Philip Harless I. and both of whom are mentioned by Philip Harless I. in his will 1772. This letter reveals also that a pastor had baptized her in her childhood and that there was a Lutheran pastor in the year 1788, of the Sacred Lutheran Congregation. These pastors either went from the German Settlements of Peaked Mountain, of now Rockingham County or that they came from the German Settlement near Haw River North Carolina, where there was a Union Church between the German Reformed and the Lutheran Churches, built by the Trollingers and others about 1755, as elsewhere cited.

For the next definite date, see Baptismal list appended herewith. The first entry being 1793.

A. B. Faust, elsewhere mentioned, in his works on the German People in the United States, Vol. 1, p 198 has the following statement which gives the next definite pastor of St. Peter's Lutheran Church:—"In 1795 or thereabouts Dr. George Daniel Flohr was pastor of the German Settlement on New River."

For definite data concerning St. Peter's Church for about eighty years, beginning with 1795 we are indebted to the Rev. William E. Hubbert, who as pastor was the last to preach in the old St. Peter's Church before it was finally torn down, having given birth to several congregations; and we are also indebted to the Rev. S. C. Ballentine present pastor of the new St. Peter's located about two and one-half miles from the site of the old church, and of Luther Memorial and Mt. Tabor Churches, all offspring of Old St. Peter's Church. The records in the hands of Mr. Ballentine are, however incomplete, but run from 1796 to 1840. The Constitution was adopted October 16th, 1796, and signed by the Rev. Wolfgang Fried Augustine Daser, as pastor, and who served as such till June 1, 1800. On pages 58-60 of the Church Record Book, the Constitution is in English, translated by, or at the request of Mr. Hubbert.

Here follows Section One,

Title, Regulations and Laws.

After giving the pledge of members to observe the rules and regulations of the congregation, it presents thirteen sections, viz:—

1—The Confession of Faith and Practice.
2—The Qualifications for Membership.
3—Provided for stated services and Catechetical Instruction.
4—Obligation to finish the Church then building, and to keep same in good repair.
5—The necessary qualifications for said pastor of the Church.
6—The several Duties of the Pastor specified.
7—The Lay Officers of the Congregation and their Duties.
8—The Lay Officers shall consult the Congregation as to what is to be done.
9—Stipulations as to the support of the Pastor.
10—Provides for lot and Parsonage.
11—Subjection on part of membership to a reasonable exercise of Authority.
12—Requires mutual regard and esteem between Pastor and People.
13—Concerns Amendments to the Constitution.

The Constitution is concluded as follows:

"We through our signatures, together with the accompanying seal. Done this 16th day of October 1796.
(L. S.) W. F. A. Daser, A. M.
P. T. Prediger Daselbst.

Mr. Hubbard says that the Mr. Daser went from Orangeburg District, South Carolina, into the pastorate of St. Peter's Church. There is such a district in North Carolina and it included the Lutheran Church mentioned above located on, or near Haw River. The inter-relationship of the German People of Haw River with the German People of New River makes the writer conclude that Mr. Daser came from the Haw River neighborhood into Virginia. This German Settlement in Orange County, North Carolina, was made by a number of German people passing from Pennsylvania "across Maryland and Virginia in Wagons" about 1750. Also Mr. Daser served St. John's Lutheran Church near Wytheville in connection with St. Peter's, making his residence at the former Church. Though living some distance from St. Peter's, about fifty miles, it is said he rarely missed an appointment. The degree Master of Arts indicates by that fact that he was an educated man. His body is likely lying in the Church Cemetery of St. John's Church, Wythe County.

The Rev. John Stanger is mentioned as preaching at St. Peter's occasionally during the year 1800. But marriage records at Christiansburg show that he was around earlier and oftener than that. He married a couple in the year 1790, one in 1799 and one in 1800. There may have been many others but these happen to be known to the writer. (See marriages elsewhere). There is every probability that he was pastor, at least in different years between 1788 and 1800. Mr. Stanger, also lived in Wythe County, and was at one time a member of the Virginia Legislature. It is also probable that Mr. Stanger served as assistant to the Rev. Mr. Flohr, as the parish is said to have included churches in Wythe, Smith as well as St. Peter's in Montgomery Counties.

Dr. George Daniel Flohr's entries in the Church Records are dated from June first 1800, just a month later than the last entry of the Rev. Daser. Dr. A. B. Fauste's statement, quoted above, placing Mr. Flohr as pastor of the German New River Settlement about 1795, is either incorrect, or Mr. Flohr was twice pastor of St. Peter's. As there is no evidence to disprove that he was pastor in 1795, we would naturally and rightly conclude that he was twice pastor of the congregation. Dr. Flohr, though a German was educated in France. He served St. Peteri's July 1st 1800 to 1823, and died 1826 and his body was buried at St. John's Lutheran Church near Wytheville. He was said to be an able preacher and a faithful pastor. His praises were sung by the writer's grandparents and their contemporaries.

The next succeeding pastor was the Rev. Martin Walther, who served St. Peter's in connection with work in Botetourt County, serving till 1828. In 1836 Mr. Walther moved to Floyd County and became pastor of Mt. Zion Church near Floyd Court House, died and his body was buried there 1843.

Mr. Walther was succeeded in 1828 by the Rev. Daniel J. Hauer, who held the pastorate till 1832. In the early part of his administration the church building was reported as being in a very bad state of repairs. Such large holes were in the roof, that in bad weather worship services could not be held in the church. Incidentally it was reported that the vestry had an elevated seat at one side of the church, and the chief function of these brethren was to keep order during the services of worship. The pulpit, an elevated affair stood in one corner of the building. This building was built of hewed logs, and of course was the first church erected on the site. It was also reported that the religious devotion and piety were at a low ebb, largely due to the fact that services of the church were conducted in the German dialect which the younger generation had, or was ceasing to use. Under the leadership of pastor Hauer the church building was repaired and under his faithful preaching a great revival broke out, and many people would cry out in the midst of the services, "What must I do to be saved?"

For the first time the Synodical connections of St. Peter's Church was given, and that it was in connection with the North Carolina Synod, and at the Synod of that body in 1830 Dr. Hauer asked for permission to unite with the newly formed Synod of Virginia. Then in 1842 St. Peter's passed under the synodical care of the newly formed Synod of Southwest Virginia; then again the two Synods in Virginia united into one body in 1922 and is known as the Synod of Virginia. Jacob Prenz, (Price) a son of Michael I. was lay delegate to the North Carolina Synod of 1830, and to the same Synod the pastor reported four congregations, thirty baptisms, fourteen confirmations and three hundred communicants.

The next pastor in succession was the Rev. Thomas Miller, this being his first year in the ministry. He had four churches, Zion in Roanoke County, Zion in Floyd County, Glade and St. Peter's, then frequently called Price's Church. St. Peter's was again reported as being in a bad physical condition, and in 1833 a reduced membership was reported to the Synod, though this may be accounted for by the shifting of churches from one charge to another.

Mr. Miller was succeeded by the Rev. John T. Tabler, but no definite dates are given as to the term he served and no special work was done. Mr. Tabler was deprived of his Ministerial Credentials in 1840 on account of inebriation. He afterward united with the Baptist Church, and died in that Communion.

We come now to one of the most interesting characters of the list of the pastors of Old St. Peter's, the Rev. Solomon Schaeffer. Interesting, because it was under his ministry that many of the "kinsmen according to the flesh" of the writer were taken into the church, these include his parents. He was a man of lovable spirit, and was faithful to the whole constituency of what is known as the territory of the original settlement of New River. Great and flaming revivals broke out under his ministry. He assumed charge in 1840 and served as pastor till 1860, when he resigned to follow up some of his people who had moved to Lee County, in the extreme southwest of Virginia. The exigencies of war prevented him from doing what his heart prompted him to do in this proposed new venture.

The fidelity of the Rev. Mr. Schaeffer in his pastoral and pulpit work was such, that not only were there many additions to St. Peter's Church itself, but numerous other communities received his attention and care, and a number of new churches sprang into being, churches which are functioning to this day, either in the buildings that he was instrumental in having erected, or in their successors. Out of the two churches he built in Giles County, a whole charge, the Newport, came into being.

At the Synod of September 1840, he reported forty six confirmations for the one church St. Peter's. In 1843, Mt. Tabor was finished and dedicated at the adjournment of Synod which met at that church. In 1846 Mr. Schaeffer erected Mt. Zion Church. This church was located not so far from Thoms Creek and on the land owned by "Uncle Sammy Smith", as he was familiarly called by everybody. Here "Uncle Sammy" was the Sunday School Superintendent for fifty years, and in the New Zion Church erected as the successor of old Zion, but built nearer the old Smith home, in which a large memorial window has been placed in the front of the church to the memory of this long while Superintendent. This old Zion Church was built of hewed logs, as were most all other such churches built in those days. This building served for both school and church purposes. This old spot is especially dear to the writer hereof for it was here he went to his first Sunday School and his first public school, and it was here that he heard his first sermons by the Rev. Rufus Smith, son of the above "Uncle Sammy." In these schools, the writer well remembers the old blueback speller and the blue and red tickets given for reward at the Sunday School for memory work.

Mr. Schaeffer was also instrumental in building, in the late fifties, a school and church building called Piney Grove, erected in the original tract of land owned by Philip Harless I. but now in the possession of Prof. R. H. Price. The building was of logs, and located towards Centennial or the Great Falls of New River. Both of these log buildings have been torn down, long since, the members of old Zion going to New Zion, while those of Piney Grove went to Shiloh Church. Mr. Schaeffer closed his first pastorate in 1862.

Mr. Schaeffer was followed by the Rev. John G. Prey, a professor of Roanoke College, which college has always been closely connected with all the branches of St. Peter's, as well as the churches generally of southwest Virginia. This pastorate was short because of the ill health of the preacher. After the Civil War, the Rev. A. Phillippi served as pastor for six months, and then resigned to become pastor of St. John's Church, near Wytheville. Lived at St. John's until 1888, and buried in cemetery in Wytheville.

In September, 1866, the Rev. Solomon Schaeffer again became the pastor and served faithfully till his death in 1872. He is said to have been born in Loudoun County, Virginia. He died, suddenly, at this home, not far from the sacred site of old St. Peter's Church. Here, all that was mortal of this eminently successful minister of Jesus Christ, was laid to rest by a people that loved and respected him for his real worth, and because his ministry had touched so many of the people and their forbears for their eternal well-being. Many yet called him blessed, but a great throng shall arise in that day and call him blessed. Repeating somewhat, the following churches were organized and built under his popular ministry: Stony Creek in Giles County 1843; Mt. Tabor, near Blacksburg 1843; Mt. Zion (old) on the Smith farm 1846, later succeeded by New Zion; Piney Grove near lower Thoms Creek on Harless property about 1857 and Clover Hollow in Giles County. He was the moving figure in the erection of Alleghany Church near Cambria, Virginia, one fourth of which equity, is vested in the Lutheran Church, though lost sight of by the Lutherans. There stood, also, a union log church near New River, at the junction of the roads leading from Prices Fork and the Peppers Ferry Roads, which ceased to exist about the time of the beginning of the Civil War, in which enterprise the Rev. Solomon Schaeffer was a prime factor in its erection. Here, then, are three Lutheran charges that cover the parish of Mr. Schaeffer: Montgomery, or Blacksburg, New River with the parsonage at Price's Fork, and Newport with parsonage at Newport, Giles County.

After the death of Mr. Schaeffer the charge was divided, as indicated. The Rev. James Turner became the pastor of the Montgomery charge (Blacksburg) and the Rev. Rufus Smith became the pastor of the New River charge. In justice to the Rev. Rufus Smith it ought to be said that he was the voluntary assistant to Mr. Schaeffer for some years. Mr. Turner left his charge 1876. The churches composing the New River charge Mt. Zion, Shiloh, built 1876, and Dry Run. This shows that Mr. Smith was pastor of his own neighborhood people, his kinsmen, not an easy thing to do, successfully. The older folks will bear testimony to the fact that he did creditable service and held some fine revivals.

The two charges were reunited for a time and the Rev. W. E. Hubbert became the pastor of the reunited charge 1876. Under his ministry the St. Mark's Church at Prices Fork and the Luther

Memorial at Blacksburg were erected, the former being erected 1878 and the latter was begun with its cornerstone laying in 1893. Under the ministry of Mr. Hubbert, the new Mt. Tabor Church was erected, as was also that of Shiloh Church in 1876. These churches stand as a witnessing memorial to the indefatigable labors of this clear thinking and far seeing man.

The Rev. Mr. Hubbert was succeeded by the Revs. D. P. T. Crickenberger, J. A. Huffard, C. N. A. Yonce, D. B. Groseclose, Ernest R. McCauley, M. O. J. Kreps and M. J. Killian. Their labors and characteristics must remain for the pen of another. Several years back the two charges were again divided, and the New River charge is at this writing, 1928, served by the Rev. W. C. Buck, while for several years the Montgomery Charge (Blacksburg) has been very successfully served by the Rev. S. C. Ballentine, who came to the charge from South Carolina. Under his ministry the Luther Memorial Church has been greatly enlarged and otherwise beautified. He serves not only his own constituency acceptably, but ministers to a large student body at the Virginia Polytechnic Institute at Blacksburg.

All of the churches mentioned in the foregoing, and to which must be added New St. Peter's erected 1905 under the ministry of Rev. D. B. Groseclose and located about two miles from the site of Old St. Peter's and attached to Montgomery Charge; are the offspring, either directly or indirectly, of old St. Peter's Church, and all of them practically belong to the environ of "The first Settlement beyond the Alleghanies" with the Horse-shoe Bottoms as the center, and in which Horse-shoe the first sermon ever preached "beyond the Alleghanies" by Missionary Schnell, the Moravian, who in a year or two later became a Lutheran minister, on the text "I am King." These churches bid fair to extend their ministries of healing and helpfulness to generations yet unborn.

Old St. Michael's, St. Peter's, Price Church, old Brick Church closed its doors as a place of worship about 1885, and soon thereafter the building was torn down. Many of the earlier settlers of New River and their descendants lie buried in the Church Yard, now God's acre, without, for the most part, markers or tombstones at their graves, but over which the mighty oaks that resounded with the praises of God in other days, stand like sentinels over the quiet dead, and say to all who pass by "touch not the Lord's anointed. No encroachments should ever be allowed upon the site and here a suitable monument should be erected to commemorate the known and unknown dead, and the chief historical features of the famous old church that served its day and generation so well under God and through its long line of honorable and worthy ministers.

We desire to close this narration of the Lutheran Church with references somewhat personal, for which indulgence is asked. As before stated the writer's father John Heavener and his mother Tallitha Harless Heavener the eldest child of Allen Harless Sr. were brought into the church through the ministry of the Rev. Solomon Schaeffer. They were graciously revived under the ministry of the Rev. David Bittle Groseclose, who had a very successful pastorate and who did much to restore the good fellowship and feelings of the times of Mr. Schaeffer. It was under his ministry that the brothers and sisters of the writer were brought into the church. It was at Shiloh Church and its predecessors, Piney Grove and the School church building that stood at the site of Shiloh that Allen Harless Sr. served long and well, fifty years, as Sunday School Superintendent, and to whose memory a stained glass window is placed in the front of Shiloh Church.

It was at the Shiloh Church that the narrator hereof was baptized, and brought into the church when about sixteen years of age under the ministry of Rev. David B. T. Crickenberger. Just a little later he voluntarily changed his church affiliation to the Methodist Episcopal Church in the First Church at Knoxville, Tennessee, while a student at East Tennessee College at Athens, Tennessee. But he has never lost his love and gratitude for Shiloh and old St. Peter's Churches, nor his admiration for the Evangelical Lutheran Church as a denomination. He gladly pays them this personal tribute and writes this word in their honor.

FOOTNOTE—There is a statement in Price's History of Methodism that there was a Church, near Pepper's Ferry called "Pepper's Chapel." I am wondering if this is not the schoolhouse building that stood at junction of the New River road by Shell's and Pepper's Ferry road? This is mentioned both in Adam Wall's will of 1796 and also in a land grant of the same. There was such a church building standing at same place about seventy-five years ago, and used by both Lutherans and Methodists and perhaps other denominations.

PASTORS OF ST. PETER'S SINCE 1876—From Minutes of Synod.

W. E. Hubbert 1876-188.
D. P. Crickenberger supply.
J. A. Huffard 1888-1890.
C. N. A. Yonce 1890-1892.
   E. R. McCauley supplied 3 months.
M. O. J. Kreps, Sep. 1893-Feb. 1896.
D. B. Groseclose, April 1897-Mar. 1903.
J. E. Bushnell, D. D., Spring 1903-1905.
J. M. Killian, Dec. 1905-Feb. 1911.
   R. R. Sowers, Suppy.
B. S. Brown, Jan. 1911-Sep. 1912.
J. A. Brosius, supplied 3 mos. 1913, Pastor, June, 1914-Jan. 1921.
H. P. Wyrick, Sep.21-1922.
S. C. Ballentine, 1923.

ST. PETER'S CHURCH, NOVEMBER 18, 1871.

At a meeting of the church council held at St. Peter's Church, Nov. 18, 1871, the following business was transacted. On Motion Dr. D. F. Bittle was elected Chairman and Geo. W. S. Kabrich, Secretary. On motion Samuel Smith, Peter Shafer and Allen Harless were appointed a committee to draft resolutions in regard to the death of our late pastor, Rev. Solomon Schaeffer.

The following resolutions were prepared, received and adopted as follows: September 8th, 1829. It was this day determined by the congregation at an election held for the purpose that George Surface, Jacob Harless be elders of the congregation and Henry Price Junr. and Samuel Cook be deacons.

October 30th, 1829. It was this day determined by the congregation at an election held for the purpose of filling vacancy occasioned by resignation of George Surface as elder of this congregation whereupon Jacob Smith was elected.

Sept. 8th, 1829. Jacob Smith and Jacob Harless were elected trustees.

May 6 (?) 1831. Jacob Smith and Michael Snyder were elected as Trustees.

June 20th. Hiram Price was elected as deacon vice Sam'l Cook resigned.

1833, July 20th. Michael Snyder was elected Elder of this congregation.

July 24, 1820.

ENTRIES

May 1st, 1831. Jacob Smith and Michael Snyder were elected as trustees.

June 20th. Hiram Price was elected as deacon vice Samuel Cook resigned.

1833, July 20th. Michael Snyder was elected Elder of this congregation.

July 24th, 1826. Recollected and deposited in hands of Samuel Cook $4.50

Baptismal Lists

Name of Child	Date of Birth	Parents	Date of Baptism
Wilhelm Samuel	22 ? 1793	Jacob and Hanna Preiss	13 Oct. 1793
T. Jacob	13 June 1795	Jacob and Hanna Preiss	5 July 1795
Anna Maria	? ? 1796	Jacob Wickson and Christina	6 Nov. 1796
William	19 Feb. 1796	Samuel Hutcheson and Hanna	6 Nov. 1796
Hiob (Job)	5 Sept. 1796	Thomas (Hobe) and Agnes	6 Nov. 1796
Adam	14 Oct. 1796	Heinrich David Priess and Anna Maria	16 Apr. 1797
Anna Maria Agnes	11 July 1797	Johannes Preiss Hanna	5 March
Catherina	10 Nov. 1797	Michael Surfass and Catharina	25 March 1797
Johann Philipp	28 Nov. 1797	Johannes Barger and Christina	25 March 1798
Johannes	13 August 1797	Christian Martin and Barbara	25 March 1798
Johann Philipp	24 Feb. 1796	Michael Schmidt and Elizabeth	13 May 1798
Samuel	21 Jan. 1798	Jacob Priess and Hanna	18 Feb. 1798
Johanna	24 Feb. 1798	Jacob Schmidt and Anna Maria	13 May 1798
Adam	12 Mar. 1798	Sebastian Hassler (?) and Rosina	13 May 1798
Sara	20 Mar. 1798	Andrews Lohn (Lohr) and wife	13 May 1798
Anna Maria	30 May 1798	Johannes Messler and Martha	8 July 1798
Wilhelm	10 April 1795	Adam Wahl	8 July 1798
Johan Jacob	Mar. 22, 1793	Adam Muller and Catherine	
Adam	Mar. 19, 1797	Adam Muller and Catherine	July 8, 1798
Elizabeth	June 8, 1798	Philip Sailer and Margaret	Aug. 19 1798
Andreas	Nov. 3, 1795	Christian and Barbara Martin	Aug. 19 1798
Christian Baugeman	Oct. 4, 1795	Jacob Schell II and Maria	Aug. 19 1798
Elizabeth	Jan. 5, 1798	Edward and Susanna Bihc	Aug. 19 1798
Johannes	Aug. 14, 1798	Geo. Preiss and Rachel	Sept. 23, 1798
Jacob	May 15, 1799	Michael Surfass and Catherina	June 2, 1799
Anna Maria	Feb 6, 1798	George Surfass Christina	June 2, 1799
Elizabeth	April 3, 1799	John Claire and Maria	June 2, 1799
Jonas	June 14, 1797	Bryan McDonald and Mary	June 2, 1799
William	April 5, 1799		June 2, 1799
Rubert	July 17, 1797	Dewald Schmidt and Isabell	June 2, 1799
Rezia (Kezia?)	Nov. 17, 1798	Adam Behringer and Catharina	June 2, 1799

GERMAN NEW RIVER SETTLEMENT

Name of Child	Date of Birth	Parents	Date of Baptism
Nancy	Mar. 16, 1799	Heinrich and Anna Preiss	June 2, 1799
James Clemens	Mar. 4, 1799	Caspar Barger and Elizabeth	June 4, 1799
Anna Margaret	Mar. 1797	Jacob Schmidt and Anna Maria	Aug. 4, 1799
Anna	Sept. 28, 1799	Samuel Harlass and Elizabeth (Harless)	Nov. 3, 1799
Hanna	Aug. 11, 1799	Christian Martin and Barbara	Nov. 3, 1799
Johannes	Sept. 30, 1799	Georg Scheppert and Elizabeth	Nov. 3, 1799
Magdalena	Dec. 9, 1799	Johannes Barger and Christina	April 6, 1800
Latty	Mar. 21, 1800	Jacob Preiss and Hanna	April 6, 1800
Christian and Catharine	Nov. 26, 1799	Adam Muller and Catharine	May 4, 1800
Rahel (Rachel?)	Mar. 22, 1799	Johannes Preiss and Elizabeth	May 4, 1800
Anna Philippina	Sept. 2, 1799	Alexander Preiss and Philippina	May 4, 1800
Elizabeth	April 19, 1800	Ludwig Preiss and Margaret (H)	June 1, 1800
Perlem (?)	Jan. 10, 1800	Heinrich David Preiss	May 24, 1800-1?
	Jan. 14, 1800	David Harlass	May 24, 1801-2?
Lewis	May 14	Sander Preiss	June 14, 1801-2
Anna Margaretz Froun	Dec. 2, 1801	Johannes Ruffer	June 14, 1801-2
	May 29, 1801	Thomas Lucas	Aug. 16, 1801-2?
Maria Margaretz Froun	July 10,	Jacob Schele	Aug. 16, 1801-2?
		Phillipp and Barbara Barger	Aug 23, 1802?
Magdalena		Michael and Catherine Surfass	July 25, 1802?
Michael	May 20, 1802	Johannes Preiss and Elizabeth	
Anna Marie	May 22, 1802	David and Elizabeth Harlass	
Israel	1802	Samuel Harless Elizabeth Harlass	

1. Bartyer Lucas. The child was baptized 6th Feb. 1802. Was named Anna. Born 7th July 1799. Jacob Preiss and wife Taufzengen (Sponsors.

2. Christian Martin. The child baptized 6th Feb. 1802. Was named (mit Namen) with name Jacobus. Sponsors Christian Martin nad wife. Child born May 28, 1800.

3. Johannes Kurgle. The child was baptized Feb. 6, 1802. Named Johannes, born May 13, 1799.

4. Baptized with name Henry. Born 23rd August 1801. Sponsors, Johannes and wife.

5. Jacob Preiss. The child baptized. Named (Hiram) Born Dec. 2nd. 1801. Sponsors Jacob Preiss and wife.

6. Jacob Barger. Child baptized 6th. Feb. 1802. Named Johannes Philip. Born May 11, 1802. Sponsors, Jacob Barger and wife.

48 GERMAN NEW RIVER SETTLEMENT

7. Heinrich Preiss. Baptized Feb. 6, 1802. Named Roppert (Robert?). Born Aug. 10, 1801. Sponsors, Jacob Preiss and wife.
8. Elias Preiss (Name erased). Ludwig Preiss, baptized 31st Oct. 1802. Named Elias and Anna Maria. Born 13th December. 18th (erased) September, 1802. Sponsors, Jacob Schmidt and wife.
9. George Zuhrfass. The child baptized Oct. 31, 1802. Named Sara. Born Oct. 13, 1802. Sponsors, Jacob Preiss and wife.
10. Andeas Kissinger. Child baptized Oct. 31, 1802. Named Anna Maria. Born Aug. 9th, 1801. Sponsors, Andreas Kissinger and wife.
11. Conrad Hassler. Baptized Oct. 31, 1802. Named Anna Maria. Sponsors, Henry Preiss and wife. Born Sept. 7, 1802.
12. Andreas Flick. Baptized May 19, 1803. Named Margaretha. Sponsors, Andreas Flick and his wife Rachel. Born 10th Jully (July) 1802.
13. David Herles. Baptized May 19th, 1803. Named Nancy. Born May 2nd, 1803. Sponsors, Samuel Herles and wife Eliza.
14. Peter Preis. Baptized July 23, 1803. Named Carl. Born Jan. 9th, 1803. Sponsors Carl Pfass and wife.
15. Michael Zuhrfass. Child baptized April 8, 1804. Named Susanna. Born March 2nd, 1804. Sponsors, Michael Zuhrfass and wife.
16. Peter Zanger. Child baptized May 27, 1804. Named Elizabeth. Born April 11, 1804. Sponsors, Peter Zanger (Stanger) and wife Maria.
17. Christian Seh———. Child baptized May 27, 1804. Named Elizabeth. Born Nov. 12, 1803. Sponsors, Henreich Preiss and wife.
18. Peter Hornberger. Baptized May 27, 1804. Born Sept. 17th, 1803. Named Daniel. Sponsors, David Harlass and Elizabeth Hornberger.

Name of Child	Date of Birth	Parents	Date of Baptism
Johannes	Jan. 3, 1804	Peter Kister Elizabeth the wife	Feb. 24, 1804
Nancy	Mar. 9, 1804	Alexander Preiss Anna the wife	June ? 24, 1804
Charles	Mar. 15, 1804	Heinrich Preiss Anna the wife	July 29, 1804
Jacob	Mar. 29, 1804	Joh. (Johannes (?) Roblinger and Cath-. the wife	July 29, 1804
Hanna	Jan. 24, 1804	Peter Behinger Hanna the wife	July 29, 1804
Sofia	Nov. 13, 1803	Johannes Helm wife Catherine	Sept. 2. 1804
Susanna	Apr. 11, 1804	Jacob Barger and Susanna	Sept. 2. 1804
Samuel	July 16, 1804	Jacob Schmidt the wife	Sept. 2. 1804
David	Feb. 9, 1804	Christian and Barbara Martin	Sept. 2. 1804
		Georg Zuhrfass Christine the wife	Oct. 5, 1804
Isaac	Oct. 28, 1804	Jacob Preiss Hanna the wife	5 Oct. (?) 1804
Jacob Schmidt	Feb. 28, 1805	Christian Schmidt and Peggy the wife	June 9, 1805
Johannes		Christian Schmidt and Peggy the wife	

GERMAN NEW RIVER SETTLEMENT

Name of Child	Date of Birth	Parents	Date of Baptism
Elizabeth	Apr. 16, 1805	Henrich Fillinger and Elizabeth	June 9, 1805
Michael Jacob	June 15, 1805	Jacob Barger Susanna the wife	July 28, 1805
Samuel	April 29, 1806	Jacob A. Cheb? Susanna	July 20, 1806
Henry (?)	Nov. 11, 1805	Henry Lope and Elizabeth	July 20, 1806
Johannes	July 7, 1806	Jacob Schmidt and Elizabeth	Sept. 14, 1806
Jacob		George Zuhrfass and Christina	Sept. 14, 1806
Wilhelm	June 17,	Heinrich Ott	Sept. 14, 1806
Wilhelm	Mar. 20, 1806	Henry Schmidt and Barbara	
	Here follows several almost illegible		
Johannes Daniel	Aug. 3 (?) 1806	Schmidt	
Elizabeth		Christian Schmidt and Margaret	July 7, 1807
Catharine		Johannes Lang and Maria	July 7, 1807
Isaac and Jacob	July 27, 1809	Ludwig Preiss and Margaret	Oct. 8, 1809
Catherine Hanner	July 27, 1809	Jacob Schell and Maria	Nov. 5, 1809
Jacob	Sept. 15, 1809	Christian Schmidt and Margaret (H)	May 3, 1810
Jacob	Nov. 23, 1809	Johannes Schmidt and Elizabeth	May 3, 1810
Rachel	Sept. 7, 1809	Johannes Muller and Cath. ?	May 3, 1810
Calvin	Apr. 12, 1810	David Lucas and Maria	July 1, 1810
Johannes	Apr. 5, 1810	Jacob Heal (Hale?) Father and Mother	July 1, 1810
Wilhelm	June 27, 1811	George Zuhrfass	Aug. 11, 1811
Jacob		Jacob Schmidt and Elizabeth (H)	
Eliza	Mar. 22, 1815	Wm. Price and Elizabeth	Illegible
Julia	Feb. 14, 1817	Wm. Price and Elizabeth	
Franklin	Mar. 12, 1818	Wm. Price and Elizabeth	
Luther	?	Wm. Price and Elizabeth	
Samuel	Sept. 7, 1810	David Lucas and wife Maria	Sept. 30
Rhode	Sept. 24, 1810	Jacob Preiss and wife Hanner	Sept. 30
	Oct. 18, 1810	Johannes (Boosz?) and Elizabeth	Apr. 12, 1811
Jacob	June 9, 1811	Jacob Schmidt and wife	Sept. 7, 1811

GERMAN NEW RIVER SETTLEMENT

Name of Child	Date of Birth	Parents	Date of Baptism
Anthony	Oct. 2, 1810	Anth. Konig and wife	Oct. 6, 1811
Catherine	Aug. 13, 1811		Oct. 6, 1811
Catharan	Aug. 26, 1811	Christian Schmidt and wife Peggy	July 12, 1812
Margareth	May 13, 1812	Johannes Lucas and Elizabeth	Aug. 16, 1812
Ludwig	July 29, 1813	Peter Zanger and Maria	Oct. 24, 1813
Johannes	Oct. 8, 1813	Phipil Vogel and Elizabeth	Dec. 5, 1813
Raph	Oct. 3, 1813	Alexander and Philippina Preiss	Dec. 5, 1813
Petrus	Apr.—1814	Georg Zuhrfass and Christina	June 5, 1814
Rut (z) Ruth	June 7, 1814	Jacob Boens (—?) and Hanner	July 24, 1814
Fany	Nov. 21, 1813	Jacob Schell and Catherine his wife	Nov. 5, 1814
Soloam	June 18, 1814	George Ferrel and Mary his wife	Nov. 5, 1814
Jacobus	Apr. 28, 1814	Abraham Zanger and Catherine his wife	May 27,
Samuel	Feb. 4, 1814	Christian Schmidt and Peggy	May 27, 1815
Jacobus	Feb. 15, 1815	Michael Schmidt and wife Anna	May 27,
Israel	Apr.—1815	David Preiss and wife Hanna	Aug. 6, 1815
Elizabeth	Entered in pencil—illegible		Aug. 1815
Andreas Jackson	Apr. 21, 1816	Alexander Preiss and wife Philippina	Aug. 4, 1816
Johannes	March 1, 1816	Christina Preiss	Aug. 28, 1816
Georg	Aug. 15, 1816	Herman (?) Herman (Seifert) and Maria	Sept. 29, 1816
Christina	Aug. 1, 1816	Georg Zuhrfass and wife Christina	Sept. 29, 1816
Ami	Aug. 5, 1816	Henry Preiss and Anna Maria	Sept. 29, 1816
Saloam	Sept. 3, 1816	David Walsch and Elizabeth	Sept. 29, 1816
Sally	Apr. 1, 1816	Freidrich (?) Barger and Sally	Oct. 6, 1816
Catharine	July 22, 1816	Joh. Schlosser and Polly	Oct. 6, 1816
Jonathan	June, 1817	David Preiss	April 1818
Georg	Dec. 15, 1817	Alexander Linkus (?) Polly	
John Margaret	Oct. 4, 1825	Jacob Broce and wife	May 21, 1820
Esther Elizabeth	Feb. 17, 1820	Jacob Harless and wife	May 21, 1826
		Michael Koontz and wife	June 18, 1826
Creed Bennett	Oct. 14, 1825	Isaac Price and wife	June 18, 1826
Hugh	Sept. 23, 1828	John Gibson and Elizabeth	May 17, 1829
Isaiah	May 12, 1829	Henry Price and Polly	July 12, 1829

GERMAN NEW RIVER SETTLEMENT 51

Name of Child	Date of Birth	Parents	Date of Baptism
Isaac Charles	July 16, 1829	William Price and Elizabeth	Sept. 6, 1829
Susan Amand	June 16, 1829	John and Betsy Surface	Oct. 4, 1829
George Synder	July 5, 1829	Andrew Martin and wife Hatty	Oct. 4, 1829
Henrietta Virginia	Aug. 2, 1829	Christian Kinser and Polly	Oct. 4, 1829
Nancy	Sept. 12, 1829	Jacob Harless and Elizabeth	Oct. 29, 1829
David	Feb. 16, 1811	Philip Olinger and Elizabeth	No record
Elizabeth	Dec. 4, 1812	Philip Olinger and Elizabeth	
Michael	Dec. 12, 1814	Ditto	
Hanna	Mar. 18, 1817	Ditto	
Martha Ann	June 20, 1827	Jacob Smith and wife Elizabeth	Jan. 24, 1830
Margaret Elizabeth	Oct. 14, 1828	Jacob Smith and wife Elizabeth	Jan. 24, 1830
Joseph Hauer	March 31, 1830	Michael Snyder and his wife Anne	May 15, 1830
Harvey Hauer	Feb. 24, 1830	Sam'l. Smith and his wife Elizabeth	May 16, 1830
Mary Jane	Nov. 17, 1829	Sam'l. K. Wilson and his wife Mary	May 16, 1830
Thomas	May 14, 1829	Mich. Kinser and his wife Anna	May 16, 1830
James Thomas	Dec. 12, 1829	George Kinser and his wife Margaret	July 11, 1830
Thomas Floyd	Aug. 3, 1829	Parents	Aug. 5, 1830
Noah	Jan. 1 1818	Henry Price and wife Mary	Blank
Joshua	Feb. 23, 1820	Henry Price and wife Mary	Blank
Enos	Mar. 28, 1822	Ditto	Blank
Sarah	Feb. 27, 1824	Ditto	
Henry David	Feb. 6, 1828	Ditto	
John Campbell	Nov. 27, 1827	Ditto	Blank
Philip Christian	Mar. 1, 1831	Philip Olinger and wife Elizabeth	April 2, 1831
Mary Catherine	Mar. 12, 1831	Henry Price and wife	May 1, 1831
Michael Miller	Nov. 29, 1830	Christ Price and wife	May 1, 1831
Malinda Jane	Oct. 4, 1830	Jacob	May 1, 1831
Sarah Ellen	April 3, 1831	John Zerfass and wife Elizabeth	May 25, 1831
Sarah Ann	Mar. 1, 1831	John Kister and wife Sarah	May 21, 1831
Leona	Mar. 1, 1831	Israel Harless and wife	June 20, 1831
Jackson Andrew	Sept. 2, 1830	Andrew Croy and wife Sarah	Blank
Margaret Elizabeth	July 20, 183- May 30, 1831	Wills Smith and wife Wills Smith and wife	Aug. 14, 1831
Elizabeth Mary	Sept. 12, 1831	Jacob Price and wife Nancy	March 17,
Sally Ellen	Sept. 19, 1831	Andrew Martin and wife Catherine	Mar. 17, 1802

GERMAN NEW RIVER SETTLEMENT

Name of Child	Date of Birth	Parents	Date of Baptism
Margaret Jane	Feb. 13, 1832	Job Hale and wife Sally	Mar. 22,
Julina	Feb. 12, 1832	Peter Bowles and wife Nancy	Mar. 22,
James B. Price	Nov. 23, 1832	Henry Price and wife	July 4, 1833
Elizabeth Margaret Jane	Oct. 2, 1825	Jacob Broce and wife Sarah	July 27, 1840

Name	Born	Baptized	
John Floyd	1833, June 18	Aug. 17, 1834	This entry is not very
James Henry	1833, Oct. 17	Aug. 17, 1834	clear and is transcribed
Joannah Price	1833, Dec. 11	Aug. 17, 1834	just as it was in the re-
Zachariah Price	1834, Apr. 11	Aug. 17, 1834	cords.

Name of Child	Date of Birth	Parents	Date of Baptism
Name of Child	Date of Birth	Parents	Date of Baptism
Lewis Flavous Josephus	Feb. 15, 1834		
Liona	Aug. 8, 1835		
Dorothy Catharine	Feb. 12, 1837	Jacob Broce and wife Catherine	July 27, 1840
Susan Marian	Feb. 10, 1839	Jacob Broce and wife Catherine	
Samuel	Mar. 27, 1840	Henry Price and wife	July 27, 1840
Virginia Susan	Sept. 21, 1839	William Long and wife Elizabeth	July 27, 1840

Henry Raborn Surface born February 27, 1837. Son of Andrew Surface.
Lewemmy Catharine Long born Dec. 3, 1836. Daughter of Ephraim Long.
Eliza Jane Cook was born July 4, 1836. Daughter of Peggy Cook.
Saranah Surface was born March 18, 1837. Baptized June 1, 1837.
Sarah Surface Long born May 16, 1837. Baptized Aug. 5.
Mary Catherine Price born Jan. 26, 1837. Baptized June 3, 1838.
Mariah Elizabeth Long, Jan. 8, 1838. Baptized June 3, 1838.
Hagy Price, July 18, 1838. Baptized Sept. 1, 1838.
Osker R. J. Kister born Jan. 11, 1834. Baptized March 12, 1837.
Mandy Melvina Kister, born March 16, 1835. Baptized March 12, 1837.
Armindy Elizabeth Hardwic, born March 25, 1837. Baptized May 14, 1837.
Alphore Tabler Snider, born Jan. 30, 1837. Baptized 14, 1837.
Mary Elizabeth, born Sept. 17, 1837. Baptized May 14, 1837.
Malindy Catherine Snider, born June 15, 1838. Baptized Aug. 1.
Margaret Surface, born Feb. 13, 1839. Baptized July 20, 1839.

Name of Child	Date of Birth	Parents	Date of Baptism
Malinda Sarah	Jan. 11, 1839	Ephraim Long and wife Hannah	July 27, 1840
Mary Margaret	Mar. 13, 1840	James Long and Mary	July 27, 1840
David Trout	Apr. 20, 1838	Christian Price and wife Hannah	July 27, 1840
Eva Margaret	Mar. 2, 1838	Margaret Cook, Mother	July 27, 1840
Parris	July 30, 1836	Elizabeth Olinger, Mother	July 27, 1840
Mary Catherine	Mar. 14, 1835	Do	July 27, 1840
Sarah Catherine	Dec. 9, 1838	Do	July 27, 1840
Lucy Jane	Oct. 29, 1839	David Kister and wife Eizabeth	July 27, 1840

Susanna Elizabeth, daughter of Henry and Polly Price was born April 25, 1836 and baptized July 10th.

Samuel Rufus, son of Samuel and Elizabeth Smith, born April 27th, 1836 and baptized July 10th, 1836.

Charles Wilson, son of Jacob and Nancy Price, born February 10th, 1836, and baptized July 10th, 1836.

Baptized October 10th, 1835 by G. T. Fahrr (?) Elphona Jane, daughter of William and Peggy Snyder.

Catherine Eloisa, daughter of Younger Hardwig and Susan his wife.

The Prices in the Peaked Mountain Church Record

From William and Mary Quarterly Volumes 13 and 14

(Preiss, Preis, Preisch, Preuss)

1st Generation—Augustine Price and wife Elizabeth Scherp:
    Susana born 1750
    Conrad born 1752
    Augustine Jr., born 1754
    Elizabeth born 1757
    John Frederick born 1759
    Anna Catharina born 1763
        (Daniel and Catherine P. sponsors)
    Maria Catharina born 1765
    Daniel Price and wife:
    Sarah born 1776
    Henry Price and wife Magdalene
        Henry D. born 1759
        Adam born 1760

2nd Generation—Augustine Price (II) and wife Mary
    Elizabeth born 1776
    Barbara born 1782
    Margaret born 1784
    Anna Marie born 1786
    Juliana born 1787
    Christiana born 1793
    Frederick Price and Anna Catharina
    Anna Marie born 1782
    Sarah born 1785
    Elizabeth born 1741
    John George born 1742
    Conrad Price and wife Elizabeth
    Augustine (III) born 1785
    Frederick (II) born 1788
    Anna Marie born 1792
    John Peter born 1794
    Peter Price (Preuss)
    Michael born 1792
    Henry (II) Born 1790
    Peter, Jr. born 1794

List of Earlier Marriages
From Court Records

Philip Harless (s of Martin)
Molly Stanley June 28, 1790.

Philip Harless (s of Emanuel)
Sally Johnson, 1800.

Philip Sailor
Margarette Harless (d of Martin) May 10th 1796.

Lewis Price (s of Michael II.)
Margarette Harless (d of Philip II.) June 8th 1799.

Samuel Harless (s of Philip II)
Elizabeth Price (d of Henry D II) June 19 1799. By John Stanger.

Daniel Harless (s of Philip II.)
Elizabeth Nash. 1797 by Isaac Benfro.

Archibald Taber
Nancy Shell (d of Jacob) 1792.

William McCoy (Little River)
Barbara Trolinger (likely d of Adam II. sister of John Sr.)
Nov. 20 1796. By Edward Morgan.

John Wintrow
Mary Harless (d of Philip II. 1792.)

Michael Harless (s of Martin)
Irene Adkins. 1797. By Robt. Glenn.

Richard Haven
Christianna Shell (d of Jacob I.) 1786.

Philip Harless (s of David)
Mary Harless (d of Henry) September 10 1797.

Writer found following on a slip of paper: "Edward Morgan licensed to preach February 1787 by Richard Swift." These men were well known Methodist Preachers.

William Haven
Barbara Shell (d of Jacob I.) 1786.

John S. McClure
Ruth Heavener (d of Philip)
Jan. 14th 1813. By Jonathan Hall.

Henry Trolinger (s of John Sr.)
Atelia Cecil June 8th 1826.
By J. G. Cecil.

Adam Price (s of Henry D.)
Mary Collins. Oct. 3d 1826.
By Richard Buckingham.

Peter Keister
Katherine Shell (d of John or Jacob Jr.)
By Richard Buckingham.

Henry Linkous
Peggy Shell March 4th 1823.
By Richard Buckingham.

John Scott (Little River)
Katherine Heavener (d of Philip)
Mch. 23 1820. By Samuel McNutt.

Israel Price
Fanny Shell. Dec. 23 1832.
By Richard Buckingham.

Samuel Smith (s of Jacob)
Elizabeth Broce. July 31 1824.
By Richard Buckingham.

Peter Broce
Hannah Harless (d of Samuel)
Feb. 21 1833.
By Richard Buckingham.

David Keister
Elizabeth Olinger. Mch. 23 1833.
By John Wallace.

Michael Surface
Margarette Harless (d or Philip III.) Sept. 25 1830.
By Richard Buckingham.

William Taber and Sally Harless (d of Philip III.) Mch. 25 1830

Thomas Lucas and
Mahala Harless (d of Samuel)
Nov. 31 1828.

Israel Harless (s of Samuel)
Mary Broce. Mch. 4 1830

Robert Snider and Selia Harless.
July 8 1843

Henry Buck and
Fanny Harless (d of Henry)
May 10 1831

Allen Harless (s of Samuel)
Elizabeth Roberts (d of Joseph)
1841. By Solomon Schaeffer.

GERMAN NEW RIVER SETTLEMENT 55

Michael Olinger and
Caroline Roberts (d of Joseph)
1841. By Solomon Schaeffer.

Samuel Smith (s of Jacob)
Nancy Harless (d of Samuel)
Sept. 21 1841. By Solomon Schaeffer.

William Litten and
Mary Elliott (d of Martin)
Nov. 12 1844.

Strother Heavener and
Fannie Price (d of David B)
July 31 1834. By John Wallace.

John Shull (s of Jacob Jr.)
Hannah Linkous. 1818.
By Samuel McNutt. M

John R. Kent and Mary Cloyd. 1818.
By Samuel McNutt.

William Long
Elizabeth Harless (d of Philip III.)
July 25 1832. By John Wallace.

James Long and
Mary Harless (d of Philip III.)
Aug. 10, 1831.

Jacob L. Shufflebarger and
Phoebe Trolinger.
Mch. 27 1825. By J. G. Cecil.

Jacob Saville and Lydia Lorten
(grand d of Israel I.) 1814.
By Jonathon Hall.

Rev. Howard Crawford and
Jane McDonald. 1795.
By Samuel Craig.

John Ferrel and Katy Taber. 1815.
By Jonathon Hall.

George W. Olinger and
Elizabeth Surface. 1848.
By Richard Buckingham.

Crockett Hawley and
Elizabeth Hornbarger. 1847.
Parker Lucas.

John McDonald and
Mary Williams. 1785.
By Richard White. P. E. in M. E. Church.

Henry Linkous and Peggy Shell. 1824.
Richard Buckingham.

Jacob Hornbarger and
Elizabeth Stapleton.

William McCoy and
Susan Hunter. 1800.

Israel Price and Fanny Shell. 1832.
By Richard Buckingham.

Byron McDonald and
Elizabeth McDonald. 1825.
By Richard Buckingham.

George McDonald and
Nancy Sesler. 1834.
By Richard Buckingham.

Noah Price (s of Henry III.) and
Katherin Kipp. 1837.
By Robert Glenn.

Alexander Price and
Sarah Price. 1832.
By John Wallace.

Alexandria Price and
Mary Trump. 1826.
By Richard Buckingham.

William Price and
Katherine Long. 1828.
By Richard Buckingham.

Charles A. Neil and
Sarah C. Harless. 1855.
By J. M. Wade.

Adam Wall III and
Betsey ———. 1813.
By John Burgess.

William Price and
Betsey McDonald. 1814.
By John Burgess.

Byron McDonald and
Rebecka Huffman. 1819.
By John Burgess.

John Price and
Phoebe Price. 1835.
By John Wallace.

Rev. Solomon Schaeffer and
Elizabeth Seybole. 1841.
By Samuel Sayforde.

Abraham Price and
Elizabeth Smith. 1833.
By John Wallace.

William McDonald
and Nancy McDonald. 1824.
By Richard Buckingham.

Samuel Snider and
Margarette Albert. 1843.
By Solomon Schaeffer.

William P. Shell and
Jane Henderson. 1843.
By Solomon Schaeffer.

Enos Price (s of Henry III?) and
Elizabeth Cromer.
By Solomon Schaeffer.

Abraham Harless (s of Samuel) and
Mary Keister. Oct. 21 1842.
By Solomon Schaeffer.

William Wall (s of Adam III.) and
Elizabeth Surface. 1842.
By Solomon Schaeffer.

Robert Coldwell and
Margarette Helvey. 1840.
By Robert Glenn.

Samuel Kipp and
Amy Linkous. 1840.
By Robert Glen.

Floyd McDonald and
Jane Black. Nov. 22 1849.
By William P. Hickman.

Abraham Linkous and
Emeline Surface. 1838.
By Robert Glenn.

James Wygall and
Mary Cecil. 1812.
By Jonathon Hall.

Sebastian Wygall and
Rachel Wilson. 1843.

John Broce and
Sally Ekiss. 1824.
By Richard Buckingham.

Peter Hornbarger and
Elizabeth Smith. 1787. (Bond for.)

Jacob Price (s of Michael I.) and
Hannah Harless (d of Philip II.)
1790. Bond for given by Philip Harless and Jacob Price.

John Rittennour and
Mary Harless (d of Martin) 1791.
(Bond for given by John Rittennour
and Peter Harman.)

Emanuel Harless married d of Jacob
Seylor.
Margarette Harless (d of Philip I)
and George Williams
(Augusta records.)

Mary Harless (d of Philip) and
Jacob Seylor. Augusta records.

Philip Hafner and Ulrich Fulwilder
gave bond for Hafner's marriage to
Catherine Fulwilder. March 19 1793.
Augusta records.

Jacob Heavener (of Jacob Sr.) and
Elizabeth Collins. Feb. 9 1838.

James Harless and Nancy Rayborn.
1835.

William A. Silor gave bond for marriage of his son to Miss Shumaker.
(Augusta records.)

Jacob Harman M. 1751 (son of Jacob) near Price's Fork
(Augusta records.)

John Shull and
Elizabeth Barger. 1811.
By Richard Buckingham.

Land Patents and Grants

Patents is the word used up till the Revolution; after that grants. These are given for purposes of locating parties and to give dates. The first patent for old Augusta County is dated June 29, 1739. It is also significant that many of the earlier patents for the county are in and around the New River Settlement. The "A" means acreage.

BLACK

Alexander Nov. 3d 1750 250a. South Fork Cow pasture.

BUCHANNAN

John Aug. 3 1748 360a on Strouble's Creek. The records show that Adam Harman failed to pay his rental to the King of England, and so forfeited his right to the 500a below mouth of Thoms Creek. A patent was granted to Buchannan for the same tract of 500a 1763.

CLOYD

Joseph. 1788. 358a on Falling Spring branch of New River. And 1795 150a same branch.

CROCKETTS

James, Nov. 1752, 148a Reed Creek and adjoining James Calhoun. Same date with Ester one for 450 on branch of Mississippi (New River). On same date for Ester for 100a Reed Creek.

CALHOUN

William, Oct. 21, 1752. 350a Reed Creek. Ezekiel, Oct. 21, 1752, 500a Reed Creek. James, Nov. 7, 1752. 610a Reed Creek. Patrick, Nov. 7, 1752. 139a branch of New River.

DOCHERTY

William, (Nov. 3, 1750. 285a cow pasture. (Likely his son or grandson who built Harless "mansion" 1800.)

DRAPER

John, Aug. 24, 1752. 270a Hazel Draft waters of New River.

HARLESS

"Michael" July 2, shows two, one for 630a and 113a on waters of Wood's River." Voided by Court 1760. Philip, Oct. 31, 1765, both above tracts patented to Philip. But in the 630 tract Michael Price was joint owner, his share being deeded to Michael Price, stipulating that Price was not to hold Harless "if the patent fails." Philip I. Aug. 27, 1770. 400a adjoining own patent land. Same date, 80a south side Given Mill run, and "joining his patent." Philip II, 1793. 22a Thoms Creek. August 19, 1794. 45a Thoms Creek "Adjoining own and land of George Shepherd." Henry, August 19, 1794. 107a southside New River (near Pepper's Ferry). And 1795, 52a on Thoms Creek adjoining Buchannan's land and one 30a Lick Run. Philip II. 1801, two 35a and 64a on Thoms Creek adjoining own land. Martin 1804 100a Clover Hollow. David, 1805. 100a Thoms Creek. Philip (son of Martin) 1807, 70a south side Sinking Creek. Edward, 1809, 45a Clover Hollow "joining land of Ferdinand Harless." Patrick (son of Martin) 1785, Sinking Creek. Ferdinand, 1803, 245a Clover Hollow.

HARMANS

JACOB—Oct. 30, 1752, took out first patent for the famous Horse-Shoe. It calls for 985a (clearly a miscalculation, as it is claimed to contain about 3000a.) The bounds as follows: "Beginning at ADAM HARMAN'S FORD at a black oak and iron wood trees on the bank of the river, thence East 270 poles and across a neck of land to a white oak and black oak on the bank of said river, near a fall in the river, thence down the several courses 2094 poles to the beginning." And the purposes named in the patent were: "fishing, hunting, hawking, fording and all other profits." (This same statement touching purposes will be found in all of the patents about the Horse-shoe). On August 22, 1753 he took one for 160a on branch of New River called Neck Creek.

ADAM—Nov. 7, 1752. 500a and bounded as follows: "Beginning at a hickory and white oak at mouth of Thoms Creek, running thence north 31 degrees, east 26 poles to a black oak and dogwood, thence North 41 degrees East 86 poles to a black oak and white oak, thence North 60 degrees, East 140 poles to two black oaks, thence North 55 degrees, West 76 poles across Thoms Creek to a white oak, thence South 112 poles to three white oaks on a branch, thence South 68 degrees, West 303 poles to a black oak, thence South 37 degrees, West 316 poles to a honey locust and hickory on a branch of New River, thence up the several courses to the beginning." Here follows the rental stipulation that appears in all of the earlier patents. "Behoofs Adam Harman (Hermon) his heirs and assignees forever to be held for us, our heirs or assignees as of our Manor of East Greenwich in the County of Kent in free and common soccage, and not in capite, or by Knights service, yielding and paying unto our heirs or assignees for every fifty acres of land, and proportionate for each greater or lesser quantity than fifty acres the free rent of one shilling yearly, to be paid yearly upon the Feast of St. Michael, the Archangel and also cultivating and improving three acres and improving part of every fifty acres of the tract." The stipulation is further made that if payment is not made at a given time the patent (and all such) were voided automatically.

ADAM— took patent for 116a Walker's Creek, July 3, 1794. (This may mean Adam Jr.)

HEAVENER (Hevenner in pats.)

PHILIP—April 8, 1799, 390a "assignee of Henry T. Stobaugh a certain tract on Little Sinking Spring, waters of New River. 290a, a part thereof, conveyed to Henry Stoughbaugh by deed of Henry Patton and Isaac Hardwin, executors of Adam Wagoner, deceased, and which was granted to said Wagoner by patent, Sept. 1, 1785; and 110 acres residue taken (by virtue of Land Office Treasury Warrant, Nov. 1732) Dec. 1795, bounded: Beginning at three white oaks, at the head of a spring (corner to the deeded) and with the line South 50 degrees, East 1130 poles to a white oak on the top of a ridge, South 41 degrees, East 70 poles to a red oak and white ash on a ridge near the wagon road, South 70 degrees, East 190 poles to a red oak and double walnut on a hillside, South 40 degrees, West 155 poles to a red oak and white oak in a hollow, thence leaving said line North 87 degrees, West 212 poles to two red oaks corner of said Stoughbaugh's patented lands, North 182 degrees, West 140 poles to a red oak and white oak by a branch, north 20 degrees, West 70 poles to four white oaks by a path and North 27 degrees, East 110 poles to the beginning. Signed by Governor James Wood and delivered to Gordon Cloyd. Following record at Christianburg, that Philip Heavener, made deed, 1804 to Adam Hance for 1000a "lying at head waters of Bullock Pen Branch" for $1000. This tract was just west of Newbourn; and was surveyed for David Croach, May 24, 1799.

HORNBARGER (Hahnbergh)

Peter 1809, 115a Beaver Dam Creek of Little River. Daniel—1832, 37a Crab Creek and 1840, 220a Strouble's Creek.

HUDDLE

John 1796, 106a Reed Creek and "adjoining his old survey."

INGLE

William had a number of grants on New River and began with 1783.

LUCAS

John, July 3, 1787, 56a Sinking Creek. 1795, 300a Spruce Run. Parker, 1795, 50a Sinking Creek. William, 1800, 270a and 1809, 200a both on Sinking Creek.

July 3, 1787, John took one for 56a and 1795, 300a on Spruce Run. David and Parker, 1795a Sinking Creek. William

McCLURE

At headwaters of 1824 of Catawba.

McCOY

Richard, July 3, 1794, 67a on branch of New River. 400a narrows of New River. George, 1815, 40a East side New River, and "joining land survey of Michael McCoy." Samuel, 1800, 55a Burke's Run of Little River. John, 1785, 100a Chestnut Creek branch of New River.

McDONALD

Edward, August 22, 1753, 200a on waters of Roanoke branch of Buffalo Creek.

PATTON

James Patton is linked with John Lewis, taking their first June 30, 1743, 600a Elk Creek branch of Cowpasture River. James took another Sept. 20, 1748, 150a branch of James River. Same date, 183a North Fork Roanoke River. April 9, 1749, four about 1100a James River. Aug. 22, 1753, 700a branch of New River, "place called Camper's ground in valley of Content," and on same date, 400a Crab Creek. June 20, 1753, 900a Thorn Spring branch; another for 4000a branch of Woods River; another of 7500 "West of a ridge dividing waters of New River from waters of Roanoke River." On Nov. 3, 1750, James Patton took out 96 patents for various acreage and at various places but mostly on Craig and Catawba Creeks and Mercer's Run. On same date, 4500 "on waters of New River, near Peaked Mountain" (near Pulaski City.) The patent elsewhere mentioned of 120,000 acres cannot be found, but that statement likely originated from a total acreage of all patents.

PEPPER

James, 1786, 200a South side of New River.

PRICES

Feb. 2, 1754, James Patton sold to Henry, Daniel and Augustine Price 1130a "on Thoms Creek" (lies between Price's Fork and Old St.Peter's. This from Augusta records.)

Michael, July 5, 1786, 25a "assignee of William Preston, joined land of Henry. Same date, 75a on New River, joining Henry. John (son of Michael), Feb. 20, 1793, 165a on Thoms Creek (Mill site), and assignee of Michael. Henry Jr., Feb. 22, 1793, 35a Strouble's Creek below Michael's, Christian, Feb. 22, 1793, 85a on Strouble's Creek. Henry, same date, joins land of Michael and John Price and Jacob Smith. David, 1800, 170a Strouble's Creek, and adjoining his mill survey. Henry, 1800, 145a "on head of Thoms Creek." Christian, 1800, 43a Sinking Creek, and same date, 150a Knob Mountain, Sinking Creek. Alexander, 1800, 300a head of Thoms Creek. Lewis, 1801, 690a, Sinking Creek. David, 1803, two 150a and 1167a Sinking Creek. David, 1809, 120a Sinking Creek. Same, 1813, two Sinking Creek, 224a and 200a Sinking Creek. Alexander, 1815, 92a north side of Thoms Creek.

SHELL (Scholl)

Jacob, June 30, 1794, 404a East side New River, both sides of Fishing Run branch and adjoining land Richard McCoy. Christian, July 15, 1795, 250a Blue Stone River. Jacob, July 16, 1795, 90a Blue Stone River and two 370a Strouble's Creek and joins Pepper's land, and 1789, 80a on branch of New River.

SIFFORD

George, 1746. Original copy in hands of relatives.

SILER

Henry, June 1, 1750, 191a, branch of Shenandoah. (Peaked Mountain).

SMITH

Jacob, 1785, through William Preston, 280a both sides of Sinking Creek.

SCOTT

John, 1783, 133a both sides New River. 1813, 30a Beaver Dam Creek branch of New River.

STROUGHBAUGH

Henry, 1793, 315a waters of Sinking Spring branch of New River.

SNIDER

Nicholas, 1797, Blue Spring branch of Cripple Creek.

TRIGG

Abraham, 1797, 60a Thoms Creek, adjoining land of Philip and Henry Harless.

TROLINGER

Henry, 1787, 275a "beginning at head of a spring," 1788, 75a, 200a, 39a and 100a, adjoining own place.

WALL

Adam, 1752, 150a North side New River. Adam, 1800, 240a both sides Strouble's Creek, joining his land and John Wall and Michael Price. Adam, 1795, 100a on branch of New River, and including a school house and spring near the forks of Pepper's Ferry road, and corners with Jacob Shull. Conrad, 1794, 67a on branch of New River.

WILLIAMS

George, 1793, 370a and 63a and 30a on Sinking Creek.

WASHINGTON

George: "Fincastle County, took 69a Dec. 15, 1772, 10,990a, two miles above the confluence of the Great Kanawa and Ohio Rivers". This tract of land is on record at Christiansburg, Virginia.

Some Additional Family History

The history of many of the earlier settlers of New River and of their progeny appear in the historical chapters, especially the German Pioneers, the History of St. Peter's Lutheran Church and the baptismal lists of the same church and the Prices of the Peaked Mountain Church; as also in list of early marriages and Land Patents and Grants. The reason other family trees do not appear is because the facts as to lineage are not known to the writer.

HARLESS

Variations in the earlier lists give the name as Herlos, Herlash, Horlas, Herlass, and Herlos. The name in German is Horlass (the o having two dots over it—"umlach —and which gives the sound of the "o" as if it were nearly a short "e", and "a" broad as if almost an "o". The name is common in Germany today, and Anglocised by German writers as Harless. After extensive search the writer is convinced that all the Harlesses in the United States are descendents of one Philip who landed in Philadelphia September 5th, 1738, and who located as one of the very first settlers in the New River Settlement. This is determined among other facts by the quality of the land he first selected. His progeny now exist in many of the Southern states and some of them in the extreme Western states. This Philip was born 1716 and died 1772. His wife was the daughter of J. Hendrick Preisch of Germany and Margarette by name, and who survived him Philip I. had land patents for over 1000 acres on Thoms Creek. This land was devised, 600 acres to Emmanuel (and home place) 113 to Philip II. and balance to David. Henry received money while Martin got his land in Clover Hollow of Sinking Creek. His daughters Margarett (Williams) and Mary Seilor each received cash. Nothing further is known of the issue of these two daughters. The names and their families so far as can be determined are given in order.

I. HENRY. Wife named Charity. Bought and sold various tracts in the now Montgomery county and moved with part of his family to Tennessee about 1800. A record in Christiansburg as of date 1810 mentions him as living in Anderson County, Tennessee, and he "appoints my son Samuel Wall with the power of Attorney". He perhaps did not tarry so long in Tennessee but went on to Georgia, and the Harlesses of that state are doubtless his issue, one of whom, Rev. Osker, is a Presbyterian clergyman and now pastor of a church in Des Moines, Iowa. Henry left at least one daughter Mary in Virginia who in 1797 married her cousin, Philip Harless, son of David.

II. MARTIN. Lived and died in Clover Hollow. Was born about 1742 and died about 1820. No will. His issue were: 1. Patrick. Wife Franky and no will. 2. Philip, married Molly Stanley. No will. 3. Michael, married Irene Adkins. Will 1832. Their issue, Aaran, Alexandria, Jacob, Livy (Tawney) Clarry and Patty (Wahl). 4. Ferdinand, will 1840. Issue: Isaac, Joseph, Anthony, Paul, Elias, Elizabeth, Sarah, Nancie, Susan, Delliah. 5. Margarette (Philip Sailor). 6. Mary, who married John Rittennour, John Rittennour and Peter Harman being bondsmen. This Mary is mentioned as being baptised at the Peaked Mountain Lutheran Church 1769. Martin had a daughter that married a Williams of Sinking Creek, who was the mother of John, or the grandmother of Floyd S. Williams, recently deceased.

III. DAVID. Born 1846, died 1817. Likely the second to be buried on his own place, the first being Israel Lorton, Sr. 1752, and which we shall designate as the David Harless graveyard. Left will. Wife named Catherine whose grave is by side of husband. Issue: Philip (Wife Mary, daughter of Henry Harless), was bequeathed "uper meadows", and sold by this Philip to Strother Heavener in 1855 and he with his family, Ballard, and seven daughters, moved to Logan County, West Virginia. 2. Jacob (got home place), born 1792 and died 1879, and buired at David Harless graveyard. Wife Elizabeth (Hornberger), born 1794 and died 1872. Their issue Mary (Harvey Gilmore and issue Ann), Nancy (Osker Kiester and issue Amanda Kirk), Ann (George Broce), Richard, who holds the copy of the 650 land Patent that was handed down through David, Ellen (Kinzer, at one time Kinder), and Mandony. David also devised to daughters, Rebecka (Philip Taylor), Elizabeth Andrew Surface), and Hannah (Abraham Cromer).

IV. PHILIP II. Born about 1748, died 1822. Wife Hannah (Boscher). Left will. Their issue: 1. Philip III., married Mary daughter of Henry D. Price. He was drowned in Thoms Creek, a little way below Shiloh Church, 1814 (was epileptic.) Issue Bennett, Sarah, who was a beneficiary of Henry D. Price's will and married William Taber. Margarette, married Michael Surface and moved to Indiana and became prosperous. Elizabeth (Wm. Long.) Mary (James Long.) Philip's widow married again. 2. Samuel, born about 1780 and died 1840, buried Harless graveyard, married Elizabeth, daughter of Henry D. Price, she being born 1783 and died 1853. Issue: (1) Israel, born 1801, who married Mary Broce. They lived for a number of years in Shell neighborhood on the now Flanagan farm and then moved to Texas where both are buried. Issue: Liona, born 1831. Andrew, who married Margarette Shell and Elizabeth Price and issue by first

GERMAN NEW RIVER SETTLEMENT

marriage, Mary (Henry Einstein) and Eugene. A daughter married a Souter in Texas. (2) Abraham married Mary Keister. He died 1842, and his widow subsequently married John Ekiss. Their issue Anna died in infancy and Sarah who married Radford, son of Adam Price, and whose issue were Prof. R. H. and A. E. F. Radford and Crockett Harless were also heirs of this Harless family. (3) Allen Sr., born 1818, died 1888. Married Elizabeth, daughter of Joseph Roberts (she died 1862). He married again to Mrs. Martha Ferrell. Issue: First marriage. Tally C. (Heavener), born January 15th, 1842, died 1924. Zippora, born December 25, 1843, dead about 25 years (married Paterson Snider). Phlegar J., born April 4th, 1845. Wives in succession, a Miss Long and June Dillon. Almeda F., born February 17th, 1848 (dead about 30 years). Married George Dulaney in Nebraska. Samuel T., born April 4th, 1850. Married Amanda McCoy. Both deceased. Martin Luther, Baptist minister, also State pensioner as school teacher, born November 8th, 1855. Married a Miss Brown, a descendant of an early Brown family, North Fork, Roanoke. Both living. James Wade, born August 19th, 1858. Step daughter (second wife) Emma Frances, born March 9th, 1862, married Wm. Dillon. Issue second wife. Floyd A. L., Allen I., attorney-at-law, Christiansburg, John C. (deceased), Mary Ellen, Martha Edmonie, I. R. Bittle, Margie, and Hubbert deceased). The daughters of Samuel were: Polly (George McCoy) and to whom were born Mrs. Francis McCoy and Mrs. Lewis Ekiss; Hannah (Peter Broce); Mahalia (Thomas Lucas went to Kentucky; Elizabeth (John Harless son of Henry and lived in Summers County, W. Va.), son Napoleon; Julia (Allen McCoy) lived awhile in Michigan and went farther West and no further word; Sarah (George Key, Mo.); Nancy (Samuel Smith). 3. Daniel, likely the youngest son of Philip II, as in the will it was devised that Daniel was to have the "mansion" (still standing and built 1802 by Wm. Docherty. He married Elizabeth Nash. Their known issue: (1) Henry (and his issue were, Mrs. Pearis Albert, Mrs. Geo. Albert, Mrs. Hulda Graves, James, Daniel, killed during Civil War. Elizabeth, daughter of Samuel Harless, married John, son also of Daniel Sr. The daughters of Philip II were: Hannah (Big Jake Price, son of Michael I. Margarette (Peggy) who was wife of Lewis Price, son of Michael II. Elizabeth (Jacob Smith. See Church Letter of), and Mary, who married John Wintrow. For issue of Peggy and Hannah, see Michael Price family.

V. EMMANUEL. Son Philip I, who was bequeathed 600 acres and the home site. This was later sold by him to Philip II, balance payment being made to Emmanuel's heirs about 1812. He married Elizabeth, daughter of Jacob Seilor. Left will. Issue:

Philip, who married Sally Johnson. (This is the Philip Harless that sold farm near Beaver Dam to Henry D. Price who devised same to his son Henry). Daughters of Emmanuel were Eva, who married George Fulzer and Elizabeth married George Shepherd. The will of Philip Harless I. shows that he had two daughters only. Margarette, who married George Willhelm (Williams), and Mary, who married Jacob Seilor. This Jacob and Mary Seilor are parents likely of above wife of Emmanuel Harless.

HEAVENER

For variations in the name this one must have the prize. The original or German name is Hofner (two dotts over the "O"—umlach—and its nearest approach in English is a tone about half-way between short "E" and long "A", or more nearly "Herfner". The name has been Anglocised into Hefner, Heffner, Heffenner, Hafner, Haffner, Haffenner, Hevner, Hevener, Hevenner, Havner, Havener, Havenner, Heavner, Heavener, Heavenner, Hivenner. The nearest of all these to the original in sound is Hefner, or Hevner. That the "v" was soon substituted for the "f" is easily accountetd for, for in German the two are sounded as if almost alike. The writer's great great grandfather has his name to his will as "Hevner". Gordon Cloyd has it in land patent at Richmond as "Hevenner", while in the court record of 1815 at Christiansburg, it is "Hivenner". The Hofner's of North Carolina have the name Anglocised both Hefner and Heavener, as well as Havener. While those of the region of Staunton and portions of West Virginia have it almost invariably Heavener. That in the days of Philip it was pronounced "Heavener" as if "er" was added to "Heaven" cannot be questioned, and further there was beginning to be a change in the sound of the first syllable by 1815. That the name as now spelled should be pronounced as "er" to "Heaven" is by all others of the name, and also by a number of genealogists to whom the name has been submitted for pronounciation.

The tradition of our family is that Philip had a brother near Staunton, one in North Carolina, and that a brother by name of Jacob died in Norfolk, Virginia, in the War of 1812. Now Nicholas Hofner landed in Philadelphia 1738 and located in vicinity of Staunton, and the tradition of his descendants is that Nicholas had another brother farther up the Valley of whom they knew nothing. And there are several Hofners in the early records of North Carolina. So that traditions dovetail. Johan Philip Hofner landed in Philadelphia, 1752, and located in Pennsylvania for several years. He evidently was not married while in Pennsylvania and lived in Bedford County, selling his farm in that County, 1786. No wife's name to this deed. He came to Virginia somewhere about 1790. The marriage, elsewhere quoted of one Philip Hafner who gave bond, 1793, for his marriage to Catherine, daughter of Ulrich Fulwilder, is almost beyond question, our great great grandfather. For when he made his will 1804 all of his children were minors, Jacob being the oldest, born 1794. The only thing against this conclusion is that Philip's wife as named in the will is "Martha". But the situation is about thus: her full name was "Martha Catherine", and her nickname, Patty, by which she was always called. She made a deed of 1815 and signed her name "Patty Heavener".

Philip's will was executed and recorded 1804 and his administrators were his neighbors, William Ingle and Gordon Cloyd. He devised a number of slaves, one of whom by name of "Michael" came into the hands of Strother. He provided for the education of his children. His issue were Jacob, born 1794, married Polly Trolinger 1815, and died 1818. They left two small boys, Strother and Jacob. Strother, born 1818, died 1896 and buried on Thoms Creek. He married 1834, Fanny, daughter of David B. Price, and their issue were: John and Henry, twins, born April 15, 1835, Henry married Naomi Bowers and John, Tally Harless; Malinda 31, 1837 (married John Matt Price 1862); Mary, July 30, 1839 (married Frank Keister 1865); Floyd, September 13th, 1841; Nancy, July 8th, 1843 (married Henry Keister 1863); William, February 4th, 1846 (married Hulda Long); Oney, February 25th, 1848; James, July 1st, 1850, died 1916 (married Emma Surface); Harvey, August 19th, 1853. All deceased. All that were married left issue. Strother married second time about 1880 to Mrs. Polly Whit. Jacob, the other son of Jacob Sr., born 1819, married 1836. In this case the unusual thing happened. The certificate of his marriage was found. "I certify that I celebrated the rites of matrimony between Jacob Heavener and Elizabeth Collins of Montgomery County, on the 9th day of February, 1836. Robert Glenn, Minister of the Gospel." This couple went to Indian Territory about 1845. Jacob and his oldest son William were hung by the "Jay Hawkers" in the mountains near Heavener, Oklahoma, 1863, because Union sympathizers. Heavener, Oklahoma, is now a town of some five thousand people and was named for Jacob's widow and son Joseph who built the first house there. Besides William they had eight other sons and one daughter who lived at Heavener. Steven lives at Homes, Oklahoma. The other sons of Philip, David and John, died as minors, the former dying 1816, and the latter, 1817. Thus it will be seen that all Philip's sons died young. The daughters are noted elsewhere among the marriages. Nothing is known to the writer further of their movements or families.

HORNBARGER (Hahnberger)

The settlers by this name are to be found, both in the Peaked Mountain Settlement and New River Settlement. That of New River was Jacob. Jacob and his wife Elizabeth landed in Philadelphia 1737 and soon thereafter located in the vicinity of Vickars. Their issue were: Jacob Jr., and Peter. Peter left will 1856. His issue: Daniel (issue of Daniel-Elizabeth Hawley, 9 children and grandmother of Dean H. L. Price) 2 Peggy Zinglin. 3 Daniel. 4 Patsy. 5 Parker (large family in Bland County.) 6 Peter (two sons) 7 Hiram (large family at Vickers) II. Peggy (Vickers) III. Nancy (Simpson). IV. Elizabeth (Jacob Harless) V. Polly (Miller.) VI. Catherine (married Samuel Gilmore, parents of Harvey and Thomas.)

KIPPS (KIPP)

The first to come into the immediate New River precincts was John Kipp, 1815. His issue were Michael, Noah, Samuel, George (killed during the Civil War), Katie (wife of Noah Price) and a Mrs. Custard. Mike's issue, George, John (married Nannie Smith) Joe (killed by railway) and Robert who married Alma Pepper.

McCOY (McKay)

The McCoys located near the great falls of New River, now the extreme western part of now Montgomery County are descendants of the McKays, who were among the first to come into the lower Valley of Virginia. Robert McKay is the first perhaps to have a will recorded in Augusta County, 1746. He devised to sons, Robert, James, Zachariah, and Moses. That the McCoys are such descendants is determined by a will which bequeaths to several McKays and to two McCoys, the McCoys being placed in parenthesis. The change from Kay to Coy is easily accounted for when you get the Scotch pronounciation of the former word. The "A" is broad and sounded as if an "O" and the "Y" forming almost another syllable.

Just when Richard McCoy first came into the New River Settlement cannot be determined. It must be by 1760 for he held good hunting grounds which would have been pre-empted if he had gone in later. His will was executed in 1792 and the same was probated in 1793. In 1794 a Land Grant was taken out for his holdings, evidenlty by his offspring, in order to make secure their title. He devised to William and George. The issue of William were Moses, George, and Henry. Each of these sons left families. The issue of George were Francis and Jack . Issue of Moses: Amanda (Harless), Sarah Sifford, Isaac, married Malissa

Albert, George, Wilzony (Albert), Nancy (Grant Whitaker) and Thomas (married Dillon), issue: George, Francis and Jack. Of George, William Francis McCoy and Mrs. Lewis Ekiss.

PEPPER

This name occurs early in New River Settlement. Naturally the Adam Harman Ford was perhaps dangerous most of the year. So a permanent and less hazardous crossing the river must be obtained. Accordingly the road was diverted at Price's Fork and passed by Shell-Wall neighborhood and on to the crossing called Pepper's Ferry which was started 1750 by Samuel Pepper. It is reported that Rev. R. N. Price's History of Holston Methodist contains a statement that there was a Pepper's Chapel near Pepper's Ferry. If this be true we are wondering if this chapel was not on the hill at the juncture of what is called the Pepper's Ferry road and the road leading by Shells? There was such a church or school building there, not many years prior to the Civil War. The will of Wall (Adam) and one of the land patents refer to a school house, and, though we are not sure, but think it the same location. Samuel was born 1734, wife, Naomi Burke, born 1746. They were married 1764. Issue: Mary born 1765 and (married F. J. Haven 1785.) William, (married Jane Reyborn 1791.) Jane born 1768. Samuel born 1773. Ruth and Sarah 1775. George 1776. Benjamin 1782. John 1783 (married Mary Robinson) and are the grandparents of John R. Pepper and a brother, of Memphis, Tenn. John being noted as one of the most efficient Sunday school superintendents in Methodism. He has filled this position about fifty years in First Church, Memphis, Tenn.

PRICES

The Prices of New River Settlement are entirely distinct from other Prices of the Valley of Virginia, except those of the Peaked Mountain Settlement and other portions of Virginia. The variations of the name like other German people are striking and show the difficulties in Anglocising the same. We have Preis (soft S) Pruss, Preisch, Preinz, Prenz, and Price. Four of the Prices of New River were among the few that came early and direct to the settlement. These are J. Michael, Henry, Augustine, and Daniel. There was a William Price among the early Prices though it is not known from whence he came nor how long he tarried. A George Price among others arrived from Germany 1752 and this probably is the George of Thoms Creek and probably is related to the above four brothers. George left a will 1799 and his legatees were wife Rachel, son John, and daughters Nancy and Mary. They lived on Thoms Creek.

JOHN MICHAEL

Born 1719. Landed Philadelphia September 5th, 1738. Wife named Margarette, who probably was a sister of J. Philip Harless I. These two, Harless and Price, owned the Lorton farm of 650 acres (Jacob Philip Harless and Floyd and Peter L. Price farm) jointly. He evidently lived here for awhile, then removed to what was later known as the Floyd Wall farm, but being a part of a tract purchased by Michael from tract bought by Daniel, Augustine and Henry Price from James Patton, 1754. He dispensed of all his land by deed to his sons. Left a will, 1802. Both Michael and wife are buried at Wall Graveyard. In his will of 1802 he bequeathed a slave to David one to Christian, and one to Henry, a spinning wheel to wife Margarette and his "Big German Bible" to his grandson Lewis. His issue follows:

I. DAVID. Mentioned as having Land Grants in Sinking Creek Valley. Wife named Hannah. The records of Giles C. H. show that there was a Senior and Junior David. As there is a will of a David Price as of date 1858 and not indicated as whether "Jr." or "Sr." But as there is no David as a legatee in this will and since David Sr. deeded land as follows: January 24th, 120 acres to David Tawney; August 27th, 1810, 245 acres in Clover Hollow Bottom, of Sinking Creek, to David Jr.; and on August 18th, 1818, 150 acres on Sinking Creek to Henry Price. Recall further that David Sr. must have been born about 1744, or before, as he is clearly Michael's oldest child, and too that both David Sr. and Jr. deposed as witnesses in the Harman lawsuit of 1810, making, perhaps, David Jr. thirty years old at that time. We therefore naturally conclude that the will of date 1858 was David Jr. It would thus seem that David Sr. died about 1825 without a will having disposed of his property by deed and gift to his sons David Jr. and Henry, and that the Mrs. David Tawney, as above was the daughter of David Sr. The will as of date 1858 was David Jr. and he devised as follows: to Henry, John, Sally, Agnes, Westa, Virginia, and to certain grandchildren by name of Sartin.

II. MICHAEL II. Wife Ester. Left will March 25, 1835. Devised homeplace to his son Alexander "forever", and by this Alexander the same place fell to Peter L .and Floyd. His heirs were 1. Lewis, who married Margarette Harless, 1799. They lived, died, and are buried near Mt. Tabor Church. Their issue: (1) Lewis II. His issue: Crockett, Jackson and Fanny; Charles, who married a Slusser, Christian, Frank, John, Sarah, Hattie (McPherson). (2) Abraham, issue: John, Floyd, Jacob, Ballard (married Margarette Slusser), Elizabeth (Schaeffer), and Virginia (Slusser). (3) John, twin of Lewis II. (4) Elizabeth. (5) (6) Isaac

GERMAN NEW RIVER SETTLEMENT 69

and Jacob twins born 1809. (7) Elias, born 1802. (8) Anna Maria, twin of Elias. (9) Hannah (Peery). The Alexandria first above named married a Keister who lived to be 101 years old. Their issue were Susan (Snider and who lived to be about 110 years), George, Katie (Raven), Peter L., and Floyd, now living and was born 1832. Peter L. married Cynthia Snider and Floyd a Sheler.

III. ALEXANDER. Son of Michael I. Wife Philipini. Their issue: David (married Eliza Fink (and their issue: William Taylor, father of Dean H. L. Price, V. P. I.; Nickie (married Perfater) and Corlie (James Kirby). 2. John Jr. 3. Augustine (married Mary Trump). 4. Hannah (married Christian Price. See Henry D. family). 5. Polly Elizabeth (married a Grosscryss and went to Iowa). 6. Phoebe (married John Alexander Price. See Henry Price family of Henry D.). 7. Nancy (married Jacob Price Jr.). Issue: Thomas, Chapman, Joanna (Snider), Mary Elizabeth (married Price), Harriett (Clemmens), Rhoda. 8. Ralph, married a Betsey Price. Issue: Erastus (married a Surface. Had large family), Frank, Capernia, Martha, and Ella. 9. Alexander Jr. Married Sally Price. Issue: Stewart (married a Collins and had thirteen children) and Mary. 10. William. Wife named Elizabeth. Issue: Eliza (Jerrell), Julia, Franklin, and Luther. 11. Joanna (unmarried). 12. Margarette (Reed n two children). 13. Andreas. 14. Susanna.

IV. JACOB. Son of Michael I. Born near 1760. Wife Hannah, daughter of Philip Harless II. Buried, either at Wall place or Old St. Peter's. He was a delegate to the North Carolina Synod of the Lutheran Church, 1830, at which time permission was granted to St. Peter's to become attached to the newly formed Southwest Virginia Synod. His name is in the list as "Prenz". Their issue: William S., born 1793. His wife named Elizabeth. Their issue: Isaac Charles, born 1829, who has issue in Kansas, Oklahoma, and California. 2. Jacob Jr., born 1795. Married Nancy, daughter of Alexander Price. Issue: Thomas, Chapman (moved to Craig County), Joanna (married Harrison Snider). Mary Elizabeth, Harriet (Clemens), Rhoda, and Charles Wilson. 3. Samuel, born 1798. 4. Lettyborn, 1800. 5. Hiram, born 1801. 6. Isaac, born 1804. 7. Rhoda, born 1810 (married Allison and moved to Indianna). 8. Elizabeth (may be same as Letty as no birth recorded in baptismal list. Married Byron McDonald). After the sale of property to Walls the family is lost from sight except Jacob Jr.

V. GEORGE. Son of Michael I. Wife named Rachel. Issue: John, born 1798. Nancy, Mary, Elizabeth, and Hannah.

VI. HENRY. Son of Michael I. Married Ann Grissom and moved to Ohio 1804. Issue: Anna Marie, born 1797. Rachael, born 1799. Michael born 1802. This Henry is supposed to be John Henry, or the John who got out Land Grant for the land given him by his father and contained the "mill site of Michael Price I." This land is now in possession of the Smith family.

VII. CHRISTIAN. Son of Michael I. Wife Hannah. Lived in Giles County by side of his brother David. No further records available. Records in settling the estate of J. Michael Price I. had a daughter Elizabeth, who married Parker Lucas of Sinking Creek. This Parker Lucas appears in the marriage list as performing the ceremony for a couple, this would indicate that he was a clergyman of some kind.

HENRY PRICE I.

Henry Price I. was born in Germany about 1722, and came to America at the same time Michael I. did and on the same vessel, but is not listed as he was a minor. Often such were omitted from many of the lists. His wife was named Mary Magdalene. Likely bought a tract of land at Peaked Mountain neighborhood enroute to New River. He reached New River by 1745 if he did not accompany Philip Harless and Michael Price by 1741. The same conclusions are applicable to both Daniel and Augustine Price. For after Braddock's Defeat the three returned to the Peaked Mountain and are buried in the Church yard by that name, the second building of which is still in use though built 1804. There are tombstones of people buried there some hundred and twenty-five years, the inscriptions of which are in the German language. Daniel and Augustine seemed to have sold all of their equities at New River, while Henry retained a large tract or tracts of land. Henry's will is probated 1786, leaving his farm at Peaked Mountain to his younger son Adam and the one at Price sFork to Henry D.

I. HENRY D. Eldest son of Henry I. was born 1759. Will 1828. Wife, Mary. He devised to his sons whose names follow with their families: 1. John got the home place, David land where he lived and the land where Adam lived was to go to him, but the will shows that land of each of these three joined. Henry received as his share the farm near Beaver Dam bought "from Philip Harless." He devised to Christian, and Sally Harless, his grand-daughter, and daughter of Philip Harless III, who later married William Taber; and to Elizabeth Harless, wife of Samuel Harless; to Kate Shell, specifically stating that Jacob Shell was in no way to become possessed of property he (H. D.) devised to Kate. He devised to the children of Polly Server and naming them as follows: Sally Harless, Betsy Harless, Peggy Surface, Mary Harless, and James and Nancy Server. The families of the issue of Henry D. are: 1. David B., wife Mary (Polly, daughter of Jacob Shell II.). Their issue were: Fannie, born 1812, married Strother Heavener, 1835, died 1877; Malinda, born 1820, went to Missouri; Henry Lewis, born 1822, died 1861; Oney, born 1824, and died about 1910. 2. Henry III., died about 1858. Left will. Wife Polly (Surface). Their issue (1) Isaiah. (2) Joshua (sons James and George). (3) Noah (married Katherine Kipps), 1834, and issue, Matthew, M. S., and Henderson. (4) Enos (sons, Stapleton, Barney, and Sheridan). (5) Campbell (James and Walter sons). (6) Hugh, wife Mary H. Stanger (issue, Seymour, Ettie, Lucy, Sally and Laura). (7) Zachariah married Minty (daughter of Adam Price), their issue: James, Mollie, Willie, Ellen, Cornelia, Margie and Addie). (8) James Bane. Wife. Sake and issue: Samuel, Lula, Maud, Daisy, and Clara. (9) Sarah (Bob Burton). (10) Susan married Christian Olinger and issue: Otey, John, Samuel, and Elizabeth. (11) Henry D., moved to Mercer County, West Virginia. (13) Annie, died young. (14) Samuel, died during Civil War. (15) Mary. 3. Adam, born October 14th, 1796, married Nancy Collins. (1) Eliza, married Rad Fisher (son Jack Fisher). (2) Jennie (Fisher Jack). (3) Amanda (Wm. Helvey), issue James, William, Charles, Wade, Nannie and Drucie. (4) Elizabeth (John Olinger), issue, Gordon, Nick, Bentley, and Cenia (Dudley). (5) Nancy (Perfater), issue, James, Will, John, Adam, Harvey, Nancie, Cynthia, Bessie. (6) Minty married Zachariah Price, which see under Henry III. above). (7) Katherine (Ritter), issue, James, John, Nancie, Lou, Emma, Mary, Robert, Thompson, and Sidney. (8) Fannie, married Jack Price. Issue: Gilbert, William, Alford, Harry, Birdie (Evans), and Florence (Kabridge). (9) Susan, married Barton, issue William, Laura, Cenia, Sadie, Mary Ellen, and Samuel. (10) Radford, married Sarah, daughter of Abraham Harless, issue Prof. R. H. Price, and brother A. E. F., deceased. 4. Sally, married Alexandria Price Jr. (See issue under Michael Price family). 5. George, killed during Civil War. 6. Mary, died young. 7. Christian, married Hannah, daughter of Alexandria. Issue: Pearis, married Polly Roberts, daughter of Joseph. Lived in Bland. (2) Michael. (3) Joseph. (4) John Harve. (5) Barney (Michigan). (6) David Trout. (7) Emeline (Perfater). (7) Serena (Surface). 8. Elizabeth, wife of Samuel Harless (see Harless family). (9) John Alexander, married Phoebe, daughter of Alexander (of the Michael I. family). Issue: Virginia (Ann Elliott and mother of Ben, Wm., John, Henry, and Charles Elliott), who lived at the old home site of Henry D. (2) Crockett (married Kipps). (3) John (Little John) (4) Elizabeth (married Andrew Harless, son of Israel and their issue:

Mary (Henry Einstein), Eugene. (5) Henry Davidson (issue thirteen children). 10. Peggy (married a Surface). 11. and 12. Charles and Robert, died young.

II. ADAM. Son of Henry I., born 1760. Married Catherine Miller. Their issue were ten children. 1. Elizabeth, who married Jacob Petefish and whose issue were: William and Mary, twins, Elizabeth, John, Andrew Jackson, Thomas Barton, Samuel, Ellen, Jacob, and Diana. 2. William, married Anna Graft. Issue: Mary, George, Samuel, Adam, and Abraham. 3. Anna Catherine, born 1791, married George Powell. No issue. 4. Henry, born 1792. Married 1817, Mary Ann Mallow, born 1797. He died 1875. Lived in Ohio and later in Illinois. Issue: Albert, Sarah, Elizabeth, Catherine Anna, Adam, died young, Delila, Mary Ellen, George Henry, Moses Crum, Thomas Miller. 5. Anna Mary, married a Spitler. 6. John, born 1799, married 1822 Elizabeth Rhinehart, who was born 1805. Went Ohio. Issue: Henry Washington, Nancy Jane, Barbara Ann, Benjamin Franklin, Margarette, Jacob Rhinehart, William Henry, John Albert, Sarah Elizabeth, who married the Rev. Nathan Martin Baker (parents of Mrs. H. M. Kagey of New Market, Virginia), Mary Ellen and Fernandez. 7. Sarah, married Jacob Burner. Issue, Elizabeth. 8. Susan, born 1801, married Richard Powell 1833. Mr. Powell born 1798. Issue. Mary Catherine, Robert Fulton, William Lurton, James Adam, Hugh Franklin, Susan Frances, Cynthia Ann, and Elizabeth Miranda. This family entirely extinct. 9. Adam, married Susan Rosenberger. Issue: Anna Eliza, Adam Clark, Amanda, William, Sarah Catherine, and Mary Ellen. 10. Jacob, born 1808, married 1834, Eleanor Rosenberger. Lived in Rockingham County, Virginia, on land inherited from his father Adam, and which Adam in turn inherited from Henry I. 1786. Issue: Berryman Zircle and Adam. The Prices of New Market are descendants of this Jacob, also Dr. Smith, President of Roanoke College married into same family. II. George. This is a large family but scattered over Virginia, Ohio, and Illinois, some of whom were distinguished as bankers and educators.

SHELL (Shull but German Scholl)

The two first by the name to come into the Valley of Virginia were Jacob and Peter. Peter, one of the very first Magistrates in Augusta County, but who later went to Kentucky. Jacob was with the very first settlers to come into the New River Settlement. Jacob's Will was probated 1795. Wife, Catherine. Issue: Jacob, John, Christian, Elizabeth, Gertrude (Williams), Peggy (Sales), Barbara (Haven), Nancy (Taber), and Phanny (Wall.) I. John (son of Jacob I) will probated 1808. Wife Margarette. Issue: John

GERMAN NEW RIVER SETTLEMENT

(went to Ohio), Christian, Haven, Henry, Isaac, and Caty. 2 Jacob (son of Jacob I) will 1812. Wife dead at time. Devised to sister Elizabeth and following children: Polly (wife of David B. Price), Elizabeth (M. A. Taber), Fanny, Peggy (wife of Henry Linkous), Caty (wife of Peter Keister), Jacob and John. The issue of this last named John were: Harriet died 1861, Pearis died 1898, Margarette (wife of Andrew—"Andy" Harless) died 1883, Floyd born 1826, died 1902, Rev. John (in South Carolina Conference Methodist Episcopal Church South), Essie born 1862, deceased, Joe, Mary, Katie (Nunley) died 1892, and Ellen born 1829 and died 1891. This last named married Harmon Keister and to which union were born: Hattie, Elizabeth, Mamie and Georgia (married Ward) and all deceased but Mrs. Ward who now lives at the old Shell home site.

SMITH (German SCHMIDT)

There were two Jacob Smith's in the early records as related to New River Settlement and St. Peter's Lutheran Church. One of them lived on Strouble Creek, adjoining the Prices, and the other on Thoms Creek. The latter came from North Carolina in to Virginia and located first on Sinking Creek. See Land Patents. It is he who married Elizabeth, daughter of Philip Harless II about 1790. He bought lands on Thoms Creek from John Price including the Michael Price mill site. He was one of the executors of the will of Philip Harless II who refers to him in his will in these words, "my esteemed son-in-law." He died in 1852 at the age of 96 years. His issue known to the writer were: Pearis who lived to be well up to ninety years, Harvey who went to Missouri, Riley, Eliza, Jane and Samuel. The last named is mentioned in the Church Chapter as having served fifty years at Sunday School superintendent. He married first a Broce and then Nancy daughter of Samuel Harless. Uncle Sammy as he was known by everybody died Sept. 1888, aged 84 years. His issue by the first wife, Rev. Rufus, a member of Synod and who died July 1882, aged 44 years. His issue, May, Nannie (married John Kipps) Floyd and Prof. J. E. B. Smith for some years Principal of the Christiansburg High School.

TROLINGER

Like the Heaveners at first, the Trolingers were at one side of the New River Settlement, in fact not in the restricted first of New River. But still regarded by German writers as belonging to said New River Settlement. All the Trolingers in the United States, so·far as we can determine are descendants of one Adam Trolinger. This Adam has a monument in a Church graveyard at Haw River North Carolina. From this we gleam the following data: Born on the Rhine 1681, came to America 1737 and died 1776. Other data reveals that he landed in Philadelphia 1738 (see chapter on German Pioneers for data); went, with other Germans, to North Carolina 1745, "crossing Maryland and Virginia in wagons," and that they were instrumental in building a union Lutheran and Reformed Church, and that they had located on "pike leading from Salisbury to Hillsboroh at Haw River." The above monument also states that this Adam had a son Jacob who was born on the Rhine 1718 and died 1798. This Jacob had a son Jacob Henry who was a soldier in the Revolutionary War and that this same J. H. was a pensioner of the United States in 1831. He died 1844. The Court records at Greensboro, North Carolina, show that one Adam Trolinger made 1800a deed. Now, according to information received from H. L. Trolinger of Pulaski, Virginia County, John, his great grandfather who came into Virginia was a son of Adam Trolinger. John who came to Virginia about 1785 or 1790 must be the son of the above Adam II. As the mother of John, Mary, became the wife of Adam Wall II, as of will 1799 and thus that Adam III, James, William and Peggy became the half brothers and sisters of this John, so it would seem that Adam II died early in life. With this Mary and John who came to Virginia there must have come also a Barbara who married William McCoy 1796 and a half sister Elizabeth. The Land patents show that Henry L. got about four grants, 1787 and 1788. He must be a brother or cousin of John Sr. John was born 1771, died 1840. His wife Elizabeth, born 1776 and died 1869. Both buried at Dublin. John Sr. devises to Henry T. (who went to Missouri), to Elizabeth, half sister (and was willed the Coffee Pot farm), to John, home place, to Martin Elliott, where he lives. (This Mart Elliott is the second husband of Polly, the widow of Jacob Heavener. Polly died in Texas and is said to have been 110 years old); to Sally (Trinkle), to Elizabeth (Jordan), to Phoebe Shufflebarger. Another daughter, Eliza, married a Durham of Giles county. John Jr. was born 1807 and died 1883. His issue were: by first wife (a Miss Hoge) William Hoge, Henry C. and Charlotte (mother Dr. Hoge of Bland County); by second wife (a Miss Wygall) Margarette (Mrs. J. H. Darst) James T. and Mary (Mrs. William B. Cecil.)

WALL

This is one name that in sound retains its original qualities. The German and early use of the word, "Wahl."Martin Wahl appears in the early lists as coming from Germany. Though it is likely that George, Adam and Conrad came direct about 1740, or perhaps earlier. Adam Wall, I, had an earlier will than all others of the New River Settlement. His will is of date 1763. He devised to his sister Apel one half of his estate, and "to brother's son

GERMAN NEW RIVER SETTLEMENT 75

John and eldest brother's son Andrew.'' This shows that this Wahl had no issue. In 1799 there is also a will for an Adam Wall. Wife, Mary Trolinger (and the mother of John Trolinger Sr.) Issue: Adam, James, William and Margarette (''Peggy''). The Adam of 1799 will is evidently a nephew and namesake of the Adam of 1763 will. James settled near Radford. William went to California. Adam, 3d, bought the old Michael-Jacob Price place. Adam 3d. issue: Frank, and Pearis and Mrs. George Evans, all three located between Prices Fork and Old St. Peter's Church. Further issue were James and Jack located in Pulaski County, John Pearisburg, and Henry, Monroe County, W. Va.

INDEX

-A-

Adkins, Irene 54, 62
Albert,_____ 23
  Adam 22
  (Mrs.) Geo. 63
  John George 22
  Malissa 67
  Margarette 56
  (Mrs.) Pearis 63
  Wilzony 67
Alexander,_____ 21
Allen, Benjamin 13
Allison, Rhoda 69

-B-

Baker, Humphrey 12
  (Rev.) Nathan Martin 72
  Sarah Elizabeth 72
Ballard,_____ 62
Ballentine, (Rev.) S. C. 38, 43, 44
Bane,_____ 15
Barger,_____ 23, 24
  Barbara 47
  Caspar 47
  Christian 22
  Christina 46, 47
  Elizabeth 47, 56
  Freidrich (?) 50
  Froun 47

Barger, (cont.)
  Jacob 47, 48, 49
  James Clemens 47
  Johann Philipp 46
  Johannes 46, 47
  Johannes Philip 47
  Magdalena 47
  Michael Jacob 49
  Phillipp 47
  Sally 50
  Susanna 48, 49
Barton, Cenia 71
  Laura 71
  Mary Ellen 71
  Susan 71
  Sadie 71
  Samuel 71
  William 71
Batts,_____ 20
Behinger, Hanna 48
  Peter 48
Behringer, Adam 46
  Catharina 46
  Rezia (Kezia?) 46
Benfro, Isaac 54
Berger (see Barger)
Berkley, (Sir) William 21
Bihe, Edward 46
  Elizabeth 46
  Susanna 46
Bittle, (Dr.) D. F. 45
Black, Alexander 57
  Jane 56
  John 12
Bland, Richard 29
Boens (?), Hanner 50

Boens (?) (cont.)
  Jacob 50
  Ruth 50
Boone,_____ 24
  Daniel 5, 20
Boosz (?), Elizabeth 49
  Johannes 49
Borden, (Capt.) Benjamin 13
Boscher, Elenora Charlatta 37
  George 37
  Hannah 62
  Johannah 37
Bowers, Naomi 65
Bowles, Julina 52
  Nancy 52
  Peter 52
Braddock,_____ 18
Breckenridge, John 34, 35, 36
Bright, George 12
  Tobias 12
Broce,_____ 73
  Ann 62
  Catherine 52
  Dorothy Catharine 52
  Elizabeth 54
  Elizabeth Margaret 52
  George 62
  Hannah 63
  Jacob 50, 52
  Jane 52
  John 50, 56
  Josephus 52
  Lewis Flavous 52
  Liona 52
  Mary 54, 62
  Peter 54, 63
  Sarah 52
  Susan Mirian 52
Brosius, (Rev.) J. A. 44
Brown, (Miss) 63
  (Rev.) B. S. 44
  Jacob 12
  John 34, 35, 36
Brugell, Peter M. 37
Brunner, Heinrich Ludwig 33
Buchannan,_____ 57
Buchannan/Buchanan/Buchanon,
  John 13, 14, 20, 21, 24, 57
Buck, Charles 13
  Henry 54
  (Rev.) W. C. 43

Buckingham, Richard 54, 55, 56
Burgess, John 55
Burk,_____ 17
  James 7
Burke,_____ 24
  Naomi 67
Burner, Elizabeth 72
  Jacob 72
Burton, Bob 71
  Sarah 71
Bushnell, (Rev.) J. E. 44
Byrd, (Capt.) 3

-C-

Calhoun, Ezekiel 12, 57
  George 12
  James 12, 57
  Patrick 12, 57
  William 57
Callahan, James Morton 16
Callwell, Robert 13
Calvin, John 21, 36
Campbell,_____ 30
  (Maj.) Arthur 29
  David 30
  Gilbert 13
  Gill 13
  James 14
  Patison 13
  (Capt.) William 29
Carr, James 13
Carthy, James 13
Castle, Jacob 12
Cecil, Atelia 54
  J. G. 54, 55
  Mary 56
  (Mrs.) William B. 74
Cheb (?), Jacob A. 49
  Samuel 49
  Susanna 49
Christian, (Col.) William 29, 30
Claim, Michael 12
Claire, Elizabeth 46
  John 46
  Maria 46
Clemintine, Peter 23
Clemmens, Harriett 69
Cloyd, Gordon 58, 64, 65
  Joseph 57

Cloyd, (cont.)
  (Maj.) Joseph 30
  Mary 55
Coldwell, Robert 56
Collins,_____ 69
  Elizabeth 56, 65
  Mary 54
  Nancy 71
Cook, Eliza Jane 52
  Eva Margaret 52
  Margaret 52
  Peggy 52
  Samuel 45
Craig, (Dr.) John 25
  Samuel 55
Crawford, (Rev.) Howard 55
Cream, Robert 13
Crickenberger, (Rev.)
  D. P. T. 43
  David B. T. 44
Croach, David 58
Crockett, Ester 57
  James 57
  (Capt.) Walter 29
Cromer, Abraham 62
  Elizabeth 56
  Hannah 62
Croy, Andrew 51
  Jackson Andrew 51
  Sarah 51
Culson, (Capt.) Joseph 13
Cummings, (Rev.) Charles 29
Custard, (Mrs.) 66

-D-

Dalton, James 13
Darst, (Mrs.) J. H. 74
Daser, (Rev.) Wolfgang
  Fried Augustine 38, 39
Davinson, James 14
Davis, John 12
Dewart, Edward Hartley 26
Dillon,_____ 67
  Emma Frances 63
  June 63
  Wm. 63
Docherty, William 57
  Wm. 63
Donahu, John 12
Draper,_____ 7, 24

Draper, (cont.)
  George 12
  John 57
Drolinger (see Trolinger)
Dudley, Cenia 71
Dulaney, Almeda F. 63
  George 63
Dunker,_____ 12
Dunmore, (Earl of) 29
Durham, Eliza 74

-E-

Edmonston, (Lt.) William 29
Einstein, Henry 63
  Mary 63, 72
Ekiss, John 63
  (Mrs.) Lewis 63, 67
  Mary 63
  Sally 56
Ellinger (see Olinger)
Elliott, Ann 71
  Ben 71
  Charles 71
  Henry 71
  John 71
  Martin 55, 74
  Mary 55
  Polly 74
  Wm. 71
English, Matthew 12
  Thomas 12
  William 12
Evans, Birdie 71
  (Mrs.) George 75
Evins, Mark 14
  (Capt.) William 13

-F-

Fahhr (?), G. T. 53
Fairfax, (Lord) 16
Faust,_____ 4, 22
Fauste/Faust, (Dr.) Albert
  Bernhardt 8, 9, 37, 39
Ferrel, George 50
  John 55
  Mary 50

Ferrel, (cont.)
   Soloam 50
Ferrell, (Mrs.) Martha 63
Fillinger, Elizabeth 49
   Henrich 49
Fink, Eliza 69
Fisher, Eliza 71
   Jack 71
   Rad 71
Flick, Andreas 48
   Margaretha 48
   Rachel 48
Flohr, (Rev.) George Daniel 38, 39
Floyd, John 52
   Thomas 51
Fulkinburg, Henry 13
Fulwilder, Catherine 56, 65
   Ulrich 56, 65
Fulzer, Eva 64
   George 64

-G-

Garrison, Paul 12
Gibson, Elizabeth 50
   Hugh 50
   John 50
Gilmore, Ann 62
   Catherine 66
   Harvey 62, 66
   Mary 62
   Samuel 66
   Thomas 66
Glenn, Robert 54, 55, 56, 65
Goldman, Jacob 33
Gottschalk, _____ 9
Grace, Virginia 23
Graft, Anna 72
Graves, (Mrs.) Hulda 63
Green, (Gen.) 30
Grissom, Ann 70
Groseclose, (Rev.) David Bittle 43, 44
Grosscryss, Polly Elizabeth 69

-H-

Haffenner (see Heavener)
Haffner (see Heavener)
Hafner (see Heavener)
Hahnberger (see Hornbarger)
Hahnbergh (see Hornbarger)
Halbert (see Albert)
Hale (see also Heal)
   Job 52
   Margaret Jane 52
   Sally 52
Hales, (Dr.) 7
Hall, (Rev.) Jonathon/Jonathan 54, 55, 56
Hance, Adam 58
Harbison, William 8
Hardesty, _____ 3
Hardwic, Armindy Elizabeth 52
Hardwig, Catherine Eloisa 53
   Susan 53
   Young 53
Hardwin, Isaac 58
Harlan, Philip 25
Harlass (see Harless)
Harless, _____ 14, 19, 57
   Aaran 62
   Abraham 56, 63, 71
   Alexandria 62
   Allen 45, 54
   Allen I 63
   Allen, Sr. 44, 63
   Almeda F. 63
   Amanda 63, 66
   Andrew 62, 71, 73
   Ann 62
   Anna 47, 63
   Anna Margretha 37
   Anna Marie 47
   Anthony 62
   Bennett 62
   Betsy 71
   Catherine 62
   Charity 61
   Clarry 62
   Crockett 63
   Daniel 54, 63
   Daniel, Sr. 63
   David 25, 26, 47, 48, 54, 61, 62
   Delliah 62
   Edward 57
   Elias 62

Harless, (cont.)
　Elizabeth 37, 47, 51, 55,
　　62, 63, 64, 66, 70, 71,
　　73
　Ellen 62
　Emma Frances 63
　Emmanuel/Emanuel 54, 56,
　　61, 63, 64
　Eugene 63, 72
　Eva 64
　Fanny 54
　Ferdinand 57, 62
　Floyd A. L. 63
　Franky 62
　Hannah 54, 56, 62, 63
　Henry 54, 57, 60, 61, 62,
　　63
　Hubbert 63
　I. R. Bittle 63
　Irene 62
　Isaac 62
　Israel 47, 51, 54, 62, 71
　J. Philip I 68
　Jacob 45, 50, 51, 62, 66
　Jacob Philip 68
　James 56, 63
　James Wade 63
　Johannah 37
　John 63
　John C. 63
　John Philip 18, 21, 37
　Joseph 62
　Julia 63
　June 63
　Leona 51
　Liona 62
　Livy 62
　Mahala 54, 63
　Mandony 62
　Margaret(te) (Peggy) 33,
　　50, 63
　Margarett 61
　Margarette 54, 56, 61, 62,
　　64, 68, 73
　Margie 63
　Martha 63
　Martha Edmonie 63
　Martin 18, 32, 54, 56,
　　57, 61, 62
　Martin Luther 63
　Mary 54, 55, 56, 61, 62,
　　63, 64, 71, 72
　Mary Ellen 63
　Michael 23, 54, 57, 62

Harless, (cont.)
　Molly 62
　Nancie 62
　Nancy 51, 55, 62, 63, 73
　Napoleon 63
　(Rev.) Osker 61
　Patrick 57, 62
　Patty 62
　Paul 62
　Philip 8, 12, 22, 23, 24,
　　32, 33, 54, 56, 57, 60,
　　61, 62, 64, 70
　Philip I 11, 19, 23, 33,
　　37, 41, 56, 57, 61, 63,
　　64, 73
　Philip II 33, 37, 54, 56,
　　57, 61, 62, 63, 69
　Philip III 54, 55, 62, 70
　Phlegar J. 63
　Polly 63
　Radford 71
　Rebecka 62
　Richard 62
　Sally 54, 64, 70, 71
　Samuel 47, 54, 55, 56,
　　62, 63, 70, 71, 73
　Samuel T. 63
　Samuel Wall 61
　Sarah 62, 63, 71
　Sarah C. 55
　Selia 54
　Susan 62
　Tallitha 44
　Tally 65
　Tally C. 63
　Zippora 63
Harman,_____ 19
　Adam 5, 7, 8, 9, 11, 12,
　　13, 14, 15, 17, 18, 19,
　　20, 21, 22, 23, 24, 30,
　　57, 58, 67
　George 12
　Jacob 7, 8, 10, 11, 12,
　　13, 15, 17, 18, 21, 22,
　　23, 25, 27, 31, 34, 56,
　　58
　Jacob, Jr. 15, 27, 34
　Jacob, Sr. 15
　Jake 33
　Peter 56, 62
　Valentine 12, 18, 21, 25
Harrison, Benjamin 29
　(Capt.) Daniel 13
　John 13

Hart, Charles 12
  Simeon 12
Hassler, Adam 46
  Anna Maria 48
  Conrad 48
  Rosina (?) 46
  Sebastian 46
Hauer, (Rev.) Daniel J. 40
Haven, Barbara 72
  F. J. 67
  Mary 67
  Richard 54
  William 54
Havener (see Heavener)
Havenner (see Heavener)
Havner (see Heavener)
Hawley, Crockett 55
  Elizabeth 66
Heal (Hale?), Jacob 49
  Johannes 49
Heavener, _____ 24, 73
  Catherine 65
  David 65
  Elizabeth 65
  Emma 65
  Fannie 71
  Fanny 65
  Floyd 65
  Harvey 65
  Henry 65
  Hulda 65
  Jacob 56, 64, 65, 74
  Jacob, Sr. 56, 65
  James 65
  Johan Philip 64
  John 44, 65
  John Philip 22
  Joseph 65
  Katherine 54
  Malinda 65
  Martha Catherine (Patty) 65
  Mary 65
  Nancy 65
  Naomi 65
  Nicholas 64
  Oney 65
  Patty 65
  Philip 54, 56, 58, 64, 65
  Polly 65, 74
  Ruth 54
  Steven 65
  Strother 55, 62, 65, 71
  Tallitha Harless 44

Heavener, (cont.)
  Tally 65
  Tally C. 63
  William 65
Heavenner (see Heavener)
Heavner (see Heavener)
Hefner (see Heavener)
Heffenner (see Heavener)
Heffner (see Heavener)
Helm, Catherine 48
  Johannes 48
  Sofia 48
Helvey, Amanda 71
  Charles 71
  Drucie 71
  James 71
  Margarette 56
  Nannie 71
  Wade 71
  William 71
Henderson, Jane 56
Henry, James 52
  Patrick Jr. 29
Herlash (see Harless)
Herlass (see Harless)
Herles, David 48
  Eliza 48
  Nancy 48
  Samuel 48
Herlos (see Harless)
Herman (see Harman)
Hermon (see Harman)
Herrman (see Harman)
Hevener (see Heavener)
Hevenner (see Heavener)
Hevner (see Heavener)
Heydt (see Hite)
Hickman, William P. 56
Hite, Joist 6, 16
Hivenner (see Heavener)
(Hobe), Agnes 46
  Hiob (Job) 46
  Thomas 46
Hoebach, Elizabeth 22
  Jacob 22
  John 22
  Richard 22
Hofner (see Heavener)
Hoge, (Dr.) 74
  (Miss) 74
  Charlotte 74
Holmes, (Dr.) 15
Hoopaugh (see Hoebach)
Horlas (see Harless)

Horlash (see Harless)
Horlass (see Harless)
Hornbarger, ____ 24
  Catherine 66
  Daniel 48, 66
  Elizabeth 48, 55, 62, 66
  Hiram 66
  Jacob 22, 55, 66
  Jacob, Jr. 66
  Nancy 66
  Parker 66
  Patsy 66
  Peggy 66
  Peter 48, 56, 59, 66
  Polly 66
Hornberger (see Hornbarger)
Hubbard, (Mr.) 39
Hubbert, (Rev.) William E.
  38, 42, 43, 44
Huddle, John 59
Huffard, (Rev.) J. A. 43, 44
Huffman, Rebecka 55
Hunter, Susan 55
Hutcheson, Hanna 46
  Samuel 46
  William 46

-I-

Ingle, (Mrs.) 7
  William 59, 65
Ingles, ____ 24
  John 7
  Maker William 29
  Matthew 7
  Thomas 7
  William 7
Isaac, Elisha 12

-J-

Jacob, Philip 22
Jefferson, (Gov.) 30
Jerrell, Eliza 69
Johnson, Sally 54, 64
Johnston, ____ 4

Johnston, (cont.)
  David E. 16
Jordan, Elizabeth 74

-K-

Kabrich, Geo. W. S. 45
Kabridge, Florence 71
Kagey, (Mrs.) H. M. 72
Keister (see also Koster)
  24, 69
  Caty 73
  David 54
  Elizabeth 73
  Ellen 73
  Frank 65
  George 73
  Harmon 73
  Hattie 73
  Henry 65
  Mamie 73
  Mary 56, 63, 65
  Nancy 62, 65
  Osker 62
  Peter 54, 73
Kiester (see Keister)
Kent, John R. 55
Key, George 63
  Sarah 63
Killian, (Rev.) J. M. 44
  (Rev.) M. J. 43
Kinder (see Kinzer)
Kinser, Anna 51
  Christian 51
  George 51
  Henrietta Virginia 51
  James 51
  Margaret 51
  Mich. 51
  Polly 51
  Thomas 51
Kinzer, Ellen 62
Kipp, ____ 24, 71
  Alma 66
  George 66
  Joe 66
  John 66, 73
  John Henry 22
  Katherin(e) 55, 71
  Katie 66

Kipp, (cont.)
  Michael 22, 66
  Nannie 66, 73
  Noah 66
  Robert 66
  Samuel 56, 66
Kipps (see Kipp)
Kirby, Corlie 69
  James 69
Kirk, Amanda 62
Kissinger, Andreas 48
  Anna Maria 48
Kister, David 52
  Elizabeth 48, 52
  Johannes 48
  John 51
  Lucy Jane 52
  Osker R. J. 52
  Mandy Melvina 52
  Peter 48
  Sarah 51
  Sarah Ann 51
Klugg, (Rev.) 32
Konig, Anth. 50
  Anthony 50
  Catherine 50
Koontz, Esther Elizabeth 50
  Michael 50
Koster (see also Keister)
  Frederick 22
  Olive 23
  Peter 23
  Robert 23
Kreps, (Rev.) O. J. 43
  (Rev.) M. O. J. 44
Kurgle, Johannes 47

-L-

Laidlow, William 12
Lane, John 12
Lang (see also Long)
  Catherine 49
  Johannes 49
  Maria 49
  Thomas 22
Ledderer, John 21
Leibroch,_____ 24
  Balzer 22, 25
Leonard,_____ 24
  Henry 7

Lewis, John 50
Librook (see Leibroch)
Lincoln,_____ 5
Linkhouse,_____ 24
Linkous, Abraham 56
  Amy 56
  Hannah 55
  Henry 54, 55, 73
Linkus, Alexander 50
  Georg 50
  Polly (?) 50
Litten, William 55
Lohn (see Lohr)
Lohr, Andrews 46
  Sara 46
Long (see also Lang)
  _____ 24
  (Miss) 63
  Elizabeth 52, 62
  Ephraim 52
  Ephriam 52
  Hannah 52
  Hulda 65
  James 52, 55, 62
  Joseph 14
  Katherine 55
  Lewemmy Catharine 52
  Malinda Sarah 52
  Mariah Elizabeth 52
  Mary 52, 62
  Mary Margaret 52
  Sarah Surface 52
  Steve 22
  Virginia Susan 52
  William 52, 55
  Wm. 62
Looney, Thomas 12
Lope, Elizabeth 49
  Henry 49
  Henry (?) 49
Lorten, Israel I 55
  Lydia 55
Lorton,_____ 68
  Israel 10, 11, 12, 15, 17,
    18, 19, 23, 24, 25
  Israel, Sr. 62
Lowerton,_____ 23
Lucas,_____ 24
  Anna 47
  Bartyer 47
  Calvin 49
  David 49, 59
  Elizabeth 50, 70
  Froun 47

Lucas, (cont.)
  Johannes 50
  John 59
  Mahalia 63
  Margareth 50
  Maria 49
  Parker 55, 59, 70
  Samuel 49
  Thomas 47, 54, 63
  William 59
Luther, Martin 21, 33
Lyon, Humbertson 12

-Mc-

McCauley, (Rev.) Ernest R. 43, 44
McClure,_____ 59
  John S. 54
McCoy, Allen 63
  Amanda 63, 66
  Barbara 74
  (Mrs.) Frances 63
  Francis 66, 67
  George 59, 63, 66, 67
  Henry 66
  Isaac 66
  Jack 66, 67
  James 66
  John 59
  Julia 63
  Malissa 66
  Michael 59
  Moses 66
  Nancy 67
  Polly 63
  Richard 59, 60, 66
  Robert 66
  Samuel 59
  Sarah 66
  Thomas 67
  William 54, 55, 66, 74
  William Francis 67
  Wilzony 67
  Zachariah 66
McKay (see McCoy)
McDonald,_____ 7, 14, 33
  Betsey 55
  Bryan 46
  Byron 15, 34, 55, 69
  Edward 59

McDonald, (cont.)
  Elizabeth 55, 69
  (Miss) Ella 17, 19
  Floyd 56
  George 55
  Jane 55
  Jonas 46
  John 55
  Mary 46
  Nancy 56
  William 46, 56
McGarack, (Capt.) Jesse 29
McKey,_____ 21
McNutt, Samuel 54, 55
McPherson, Hattie 68

-M-

Madison, (Capt.) Thomas 29
Mallow, Mary Ann 72
Marrs, (Lt.) Alexander 30
Martin, Andreas 46
  Andrew 51
  Barbara 46, 47, 48
  Catherine 51
  Christian 46, 47, 48
  David 48
  George Snyder 51
  Hanna 47
  Hatty 51
  Jacobus 47
  Johannes 46
  Sally Ellen 51
Meser, Adam 12
Messler, Anna Maria 46
  Johannes 46
  Martha 46
Miller (see also Muller)
  Adam 6
  Catherine 72
  Polly 66
  (Rev.) Thomas 40
Montgomery, James 6
  (Capt.) John 29
Morgan, Edward 54
Muller (see also Miller)
  Adam 46, 47
  Cath. (?) 49
  Catharine/Catherine 46, 47
  Christian 47
  Johan Jacob 46

Muller, (cont.)
  Johannes 49
  Rachel 49

-N-

Nash, Elizabeth 54, 63
Neil, Charles A. 55
Nunley, Katie 73

-O-

Ohlinger (see Olinger)
Olinger, _____ 23
  Bentley 71
  Cenia 71
  Christian 71
  David 51
  Elizabeth 51, 52, 54, 71
  George W. 55
  Gordon 71
  Hanna 51
  Henrick 22
  John 23, 71
  Mary Catherine 52
  Michael 51, 55
  Nick 71
  Otey 71
  Parris 52
  Philip 51
  Philip Christian 51
  Samuel 71
  Sarah Catherine 52
  Susan 71
Ott, Heinrich 49
  Wilhelm 49
Oyle, Benjamin 12

-P-

Patton, Henry 58
  James 10, 11, 14, 17, 18,
    19, 20, 21, 23, 24, 34,
    35, 36, 59, 68
  (Col.) James 7

Pearis, George 13
Peery, Hannah 69
Pendleton, Edward 29
Penn, William 18, 28
Pepper, _____ 60
  Alma 66
  Benjamin 67
  George 67
  James 59
  Jane 67
  John 67
  John R. 67
  Mary 67
  Naomi 67
  Ruth 67
  Samuel 15, 67
  Sarah 67
  William 67
Perfater, Adam 71
  Bessie 71
  Cynthia 71
  Emeline 71
  Harvey 71
  James 71
  John 71
  Nancie 71
  Nancy 71
  Nickie 69
  Will 71
Petefish, Andrew Jackson 72
  Diana 72
  Ellen 72
  Elizabeth 72
  Jacob 72
  John 72
  Mary 72
  Samuel 72
  Thomas Barton 72
  William 72
Pfass, Carl 48
Phillippi, (Rev.) A. 42
Porter, _____ 16, 19
  Mary 16
Powell, Anna Catherine 72
  Cynthia Ann 72
  Elizabeth Miranda 72
  George 72
  Hugh Franklin 72
  James Adam 72
  Mary Catherine 72
  Richard 72
  Robert Fulton 72
  Susan 72
  Susan Frances 72

Powell, (cont.)
  William Lurton 72
Preinz (see Price)
Preis (see Price)
Preisch (see Price)
Preish (see Price)
Preiss (see Price)
Prenz (see Price)
Preston, Frances 34, 35, 36
  John 21, 24, 34, 35, 36
  Lewis 21
  William 7, 24, 34, 36, 59
  (Col.) William 29, 30
Preuss (see Price)
Prey, (Rev.) John G. 41
Price, _____ 15, 19, 24, 32, 44, 61, 73
  A. E. F. 63, 71
  Abraham 55, 68, 72
  Adam 46, 53, 54, 63, 70, 71, 72
  Adam Clark 72
  Addie 71
  Agnes 37, 68
  Agnus 37
  Albert 72
  Alexander 47, 48, 50, 55, 59, 68, 69, 71
  Alexander, Jr. 69
  Alexandria 55, 69, 71
  Alexandria, Jr. 71
  Alford 71
  Amanda 71, 72
  Ami 50
  Andreas 69
  Andreas Jackson 50
  Ann 70
  Anna 47, 48, 72
  Anna Catharina 53
  Anna Catherine 72
  Anna Eliza 72
  Anna Margretha 37
  Anna Maria 46, 48, 50, 69
  Anna Marie 53, 70
  Anna Mary 72
  Anna Philippina 47
  Annie 71
  Augustine 10, 11, 18, 19, 21, 22, 23, 25, 30, 32, 53, 59, 67, 68, 69, 70
  Augustine, Jr. 53
  Augustine, III 53
  Ballard 68
  Barbara 53

Price, (cont.)
  Barbara Ann 72
  Barney 71
  Benjamin Franklin 72
  Berryman Zircle 72
  Betsey 69
  Big Jake 63
  Birdie 71
  Campbell 71
  Capernia 69
  Carl 48
  Catherine 53, 72
  Catherine Anna 72
  Chapman 69
  Charles 48, 68, 72
  Charles Wilson 53, 69
  Christ 51
  Christian 52, 59, 68, 69, 70, 71
  Christiana 53
  Christina 50
  Clara 71
  Clemens 69
  Conrad 53
  Corlie 69
  Cornelia 71
  Creed Bennett 50
  Crockett 68, 71
  Cynthia 69
  Daisy 71
  Daniel 11, 18, 19, 21, 23, 32, 53, 59, 67, 68, 70
  David 50, 60, 68, 69, 70
  David, Jr. 68
  David, Sr. 68
  David B. 55, 65, 73
  David Trout 52, 71
  Delila 72
  Eleanor 72
  Elias 48, 69
  Eliza 49, 69, 71
  Elizabeth 47, 49, 51, 53, 54, 62, 68, 69, 70, 71, 72
  Elizabeth Mary 51
  Ella 69
  Ellen 71
  Emeline 71
  Enos 51, 56, 71
  Erastus 69
  Ester 68
  Ettie 71
  Fannie 55, 71
  Fanny 65, 68

Price, (cont.)
  Fernandez 72
  Florence 71
  Floyd 68, 69
  Frank 68, 69
  Franklin 49, 69
  Frederick 53
  Frederick II 53
  Geo. 46
  George 67, 69, 71, 72
  George Henry 72
  Gilbert 71
  (Dean) H. L. 66, 69
  Hagy 52
  Hanna 46, 47, 48, 49, 50
  Hannah 52, 63, 68, 69, 70, 71
  Harless 5
  Harriet 69
  Harriett 69
  Harry 71
  Hattie 68
  Heinrich 47, 48
  Heinrich David 46, 47
  Henderson 71
  Hendrick 37
  Henreich 48
  Henry 11, 18, 19, 21, 23, 32, 48, 50, 51, 52, 53, 59, 64, 67, 68, 69, 70, 72
  Henry I 70, 72
  Henry, Jr. (II) 45, 53, 59
  Henry III 55, 71
  Henry III (?) 56
  Henry D. 53, 54, 62, 64, 69, 70, 71
  Henry David 51
  Henry Davidson 72
  Henry Lewis 71
  Henry Washington 72
  Hiram 45, 47, 69
  Hugh 71
  Isaac 48, 49, 50, 68, 69
  Isaac Charles 51, 69
  Isaiah 50, 71
  Israel 50, 54, 55
  J. Hendrick 61
  (Prof.) J. J. 33
  J. Michael 67
  J. Michael I 33, 34, 70
  Jack 71
  Jackson 68
  Jacob 35, 40, 46, 47, 49,

Price, (cont.)
  51, 53, 56, 68, 69, 72, 75
  Jacob, Jr. 69
  Jacob Rhinehart 72
  James 71
  James B. 52
  James Bane 71
  Jennie 71
  Joanna 69
  Joannah 52
  Johannes 46, 47, 50
  John 55, 59, 67, 68, 69, 70, 72, 73
  John (Little John) 71
  John, Jr. 69
  John Albert 72
  John Alexander 69, 71
  John Campbell 51
  John Frederick 53
  John George 53
  John Harve 71
  John Henry 70
  John Matt 65
  John Michael 22, 68
  John Peter 53
  Jonah Hendrick 23
  Jonah Michael 33
  Jonathan 50
  Joseph 71
  Joshua 51, 71
  Julia 49, 69
  Juliana 53
  Katherine 71
  Katie 66, 69
  Laura 71
  Latty 47
  Letty 69
  Lewis 47, 54, 59, 63, 68
  Lewis II 68
  Lucy 71
  Ludwig (Louis) 33, 47, 48, 49
  Lula 71
  Luther 49, 69
  M. S. 71
  Magdalene 53
  Malinda 65, 71
  Margaret 33, 47, 49, 53
  Margarette 61, 68, 69, 72
  Margarette (Peggy) 63
  Margie 71
  Maria Catharina 53
  Martha 69

Price, (cont.)
  Mary 51, 53, 62, 67, 69,
    70, 71, 72
  Mary Ann 72
  Mary Catherine 51, 52
  Mary Elizabeth 69
  Mary Ellen 72
  Mary Magdalene 70
  Matthew 71
  Maud 71
  Michael 5, 10, 11, 12, 18,
    21, 23, 24, 47, 53, 57,
    59, 63, 68, 70, 71, 73,
    75
  Michael I 19, 25, 26, 40,
    56, 63, 69, 70, 71
  Michael II 54, 63, 68
  Michael Miller 51
  Minty 71
  Mollie 71
  Moses Crum 72
  Nancy 47, 48, 51, 53, 67,
    69, 71
  Nancy Jane 72
  Nickie 69
  Noah 51, 55, 66, 71
  Oney 71
  Pearis 71
  Peggy 72
  Perlem (?) 47
  Peter 48, 53
  Peter, Jr. 53
  Peter L. 68, 69
  Philippina 47, 50
  Philippini 69
  Phoebe 55, 69, 71
  Polly 50, 53, 71, 73
  Polly Elizabeth 69
  (Prof.) R. H. 41, 63, 71
  (Rev.) R. N. 67
  Rachael 70
  Rachel 46, 67, 69
  Radford 63, 71
  Rahel (Rachel?) 47
  Ralph 69
  Raph 50
  Rhoda 69
  Rhode 49
  Robert 72
  Roppert (Robert?) 48
  Sally 68, 69, 71
  Samuel 46, 52, 69, 71, 72
  Sander 47
  Sarah 51, 53, 55, 63, 68,

Price, (cont.)
    71, 72
  Sarah Catherine 72
  Sarah Elizabeth 72
  Serena 71
  Seymour 71
  Sheridan 71
  Stapleton 71
  Stewart 69
  Susan 69, 71, 72
  Susana 53
  Susanna 69
  Susanna Elizabeth 53
  T. Jacob 46
  Thomas 69
  Thomas Miller 72
  Virginia 68, 71
  Walter 71
  Westa 68
  Wilhelm Samuel 46
  William 23, 51, 55, 67,
    69, 71, 72
  William Henry 72
  William S. 69
  William Taylor 69
  Willie 71
  Wm. 49
  Zachariah 52, 71
  Priess (see Price)
  Prive (see Price)
  Prus (see Price)
  Pruss (see Price)

-R-

Randolph, (Hon.) Peyton 29
Raven, Katie 69
Rayborn, Nancy 56
Reed, Margarette 69
Rentfre, Peter 12
Reyborn, Jane 67
Rhinehart, Elizabeth 72
Ribble, _____ 14
Rittennour, John 56, 62
  Mary 62
Rittenour (see Rittennour)
Ritter, Emma 71
  James 71
  John 71
  Katherine 71
  Lou 71

Ritter, (cont.)
  Mary 71
  Nancie 71
  Robert 71
  Sidney 71
  Thompson 71
Roberts, Caroline 55
  Elizabeth 54, 63
  Joseph 54, 55, 63, 71
  Polly 71
Robinson,_____ 17, 19
  (Justice) 33
  (Capt.) George 14
  Mary 67
Roblinger, Cath. 48
  Jacob 48
  Joh. (Johannes?) 48
Roosevelt, Theodore 9
Rosenberger, Eleanor 72
  Susan 72
Ruffer, Anna Margaretz 47
  Johannes 47
Roupe,_____ 17
Rupp,_____ 22

-S-

Sailer, Elizabeth 46
  Margaret(te) 46, 62
  Philip 46, 54, 62
Sailing, John Peter 20, 21
Sailor (see Sailer)
Sales, Peggy 72
Sapsley, Joseph 13
Sartin,_____ 68
Saville, Jacob 55
Sayforde, Samuel 55
Schaeffer,_____ 23
  Adam 22
  Elizabeth 68
  Peter 22
  (Rev.) Solomon 40, 41, 42,
    44, 45, 54, 55, 56
Schaggs (see Shaggs)
Schele, Jacob 47
  Maria Margaretz 47
Schell, Catherine 49, 50
  Christian Baugeman 46
  Fany 50
  Hanner 49
  Jacob 49, 50

Schell, (cont.)
  Jacob II 46
  Maria 46, 49
Scheppert, Elizabeth 47
  Georg 47
  Johannes 47
Scherp, Elizabeth 53
Schlosser, Catharine 50
  Joh. 50
  Polly 50
Schmidt (see also Smith)
  _____ 24
  Anna 50
  Anna Margaret 47
  Anna Maria 46, 47
  Barbara 49
  Catharan 50
  Christian 22, 48, 49, 50
  Daniel 49
  Dewald 46
  Elizabeth 46, 49
  Henry 49
  Isabell 46
  Jacob 46, 47, 48, 49
  Jacobus 50
  Johann Philipp 46
  Johanna 46
  Johannes 48, 49
  Margaret 49
  Michael 46, 50
  Peggy 48, 50
  Rubert 46
  Samuel 48, 50
  Wilhelm 49
Schnell,_____ 9, 10, 16,
  31, 32, 43
  (Rev.) 34
Scholl (see Shell)
Scott, John 54, 60
Seh----, Christian 48
  Elizabeth 48
Seifert, Georg 50
  Herman 50
  Maria 50
Seilor, Elizabeth 63
  Jacob 63, 64
  Mary 61, 64
Server, James 71
  Nancy 71
  Polly 70
Sesler, Nancy 55
Sevier,_____ 30
Seybole, Elizabeth 55
Seylor, Jacob 56

Shafer, Peter 45
Shaggs, James 12
Shannon, Thomas 13
  (Capt.) Thomas 30
Shelby,_____ 30
  (Capt.) Evan 29
Sheler,_____ 69
Shell,_____ 5, 19, 26, 34, 67
  Barbara 54, 72
  Catherine 72
  Caty 73
  Christian 60, 72, 73
  Christiana 54
  Elizabeth 72, 73
  Ellen 73
  Essie 73
  Fanny 54, 55, 73
  Floyd 73
  Gertrude 72
  Harriet 73
  Haven 73
  Henry 73
  Isaac 73
  Jacob 12, 17, 18, 21, 23, 24, 54, 59, 60, 70, 72, 73
  Jacob I 54, 73
  Jacob, Jr. (II) 54, 60, 70
  Joe 73
  John 54, 55, 56, 72, 73
  (Rev.) John 73
  Kate 70
  Katherine 54
  Katie 73
  Margarette 62, 72, 73
  Mary 73
  Nancy 54, 72
  Pearis 73
  Peggy 54, 55, 72, 73
  Peter 22, 24, 72
  Phanny 72
  Polly 71, 73
  William P. 56
Shepherd, Elizabeth 64
  George 57, 64
Shufflebarger, Jacob L. 55
  Phoebe 74
Shull (see Shell)
Shumaker, (Miss) 56
Sibolt,_____ 23
  John Philip 22
Sifford,_____ 17, 18

Sifford, (cont.)
  George 60
  Sarah 66
Siler, Henry 60
  William A. 56
Simmons, (Judge) 8
Simpson, Nancy 66
Slusser,_____ 68
  Margarette 68
  Virginia 68
Smith (see also Schmidt) 70
  (Dr.) 72
  Eliza 73
  Elizabeth 37, 51, 53, 55, 56, 63, 73
  Elizabeth Harless 23, 36
  Floyd 73
  Harvey 73
  Harvey Hauer 51
  (Prof.) J. E. B. 36, 73
  Jacob 22, 37, 45, 51, 54, 55, 60, 63, 73
  Jane 73
  Margaret 51
  Martha Ann 51
  Mary Jane 51
  May 73
  Nancy 63, 73
  Nannie 66, 73
  Pearis 73
  Philip 12
  Riley 73
  (Rev.) Rufus 41, 42, 73
  Sam'l. 51
  Sammy 36, 41
  Samuel 45, 53, 54, 55, 63, 73
  Samuel Rufus 53
  Wills 51
Snider, Alphore Tabler 52
  Cynthia 69
  Harrison 69
  Joanna 69
  Malindy Catherine 52
  Nicholas 60
  Paterson 63
  Robert 54
  Samuel 55
  Susan 69
  Zippora 63
Snider (?), Mary Elizabeth 52
Snyder, Anne 51
  Elphona 53

Snyder, (cont.)
  Joseph 51
  Michael 45, 51
  Peggy 53
Souter, _____ 63
Sowers, (Rev.) R. R. 44
Spangenberg, _____ 9
Spitler, _____ 72
  Anna Mary 72
Spottswood, _____ 21
Stanger (see also Zanger)
  Elizabeth 48
  (Rev.) John 39, 54
  Maria 48
  Mary H. 71
  Peter 48
Stanley, Molly 54, 62
Stapleton, Elizabeth 55
Starnecker, Samuel 12
Stevenson, William 13
Stevents, John 13
Stoubaugh/Stobaugh, Henry T. 58
Strickler, Abraham 13
Stroud, John 12
Stroughbaugh, Henry 60
Stuart, Samuel 13
Surface, _____ 23, 69
  Andrew 52, 62
  Anna Maria 46
  Betsy 51
  Catharina/Catherina/
    Catherine 46, 47
  Christina 46, 49, 50
  Christine 48
  Elizabeth 51, 55, 56, 62
  Emeline 56
  Emma 65
  Georg 48, 50
  George 45, 46, 48, 49, 50
  Gottfrie 22
  Henry Raborn 52
  Jacob 46, 49
  John 51
  John Philip 22
  Magdalena 47
  Margaret 52
  Margarette 62
  Michael 34, 35, 36, 46, 47, 48, 54, 62
  Peggy 71, 72
  Petrus 50
  Polly 71
  Sara 48

Surface, (cont.)
  Sarah Ellen 51
  Saranah 52
  Serena 71
  Susan Amand 51
  Susanna 48
  Wilhelm 49
Surfas (see Surface)
Surfass (see Surface)
Swift, Richard 54

-T-

Taber, Archibald 54
  Elizabeth 73
  Katy 55
  M. A. 73
  Nancy 72
  Sally 70
  Sarah 62
  William 54, 62, 70
Tabler, (Rev.) John T. 40
Tarrelton, (Col.) 30
Tawney, David 68
  (Mrs.) David 68
  Livy 62
Taylor, _____ 5
  Philip 62
  Rebecka 62
Thompson, Alexander 13
  William 13
Toney, John 16
Trigg, Abraham 60
  (Capt.) Stephen 29
Trinkle, Sally 74
Trolinger, _____ 24, 37
  Adam 22, 73
  Adam II 54, 74
  Barbara 54, 74
  Charlotte 74
  Eliza 74
  Elizabeth 74
  H. L. 74
  Henry 54, 60
  Henry C. 74
  Henry L. 74
  Henry T. 74
  Jacob 74
  Jacob Henry 74
  James T. 74
  John 22, 74

Trolinger, (cont.)
  John, Jr. 74
  John, Sr. 54, 74, 75
  Margarette 74
  Mary 74, 75
  Phoebe 55
  Polly 65
  Sally 74
  William 74
  William H. 22
Trollinger (see Trolinger)
Trump, Mary 55, 69
Turner, (Rev.) James 42

-V-

Vickers, Peggy 66
Vogel, Elizabeth 50
  Johannes 50
  Phipil 50

-W-

Waddell, _____ 7
Wade, J. M. 55
Wagoner, Adam 58
Wahl (see Wall)
Walker, (Col.) 5, 9
Wall, _____ 19, 26, 67, 69
  Adam 21, 22, 23, 36, 44,
    46, 60, 67, 74, 75
  Adam I 74
  Adam II 74
  Adam III 55, 56, 74, 75
  Andrew 75
  Apel 74
  Betsey 55
  Conrad 60, 74
  Floyd 68
  Frank 75
  George 74
  Henry 75
  Jack 75
  James 74, 75
  John 34, 35, 36, 60, 75
  Margarette (Peggy) 75
  Martin 22, 23, 74
  Mary 75

Wall, (cont.)
  Patty 62
  Pearis 75
  Peggy 74
  Phanny 72
  Wilhelm 46
  William 56, 74, 75
Wallace, John 54, 55
Walsch, David 50
  Elizabeth 50
  Saloam 50
Walther, (Rev.) Martin 39,
  40
Ward, Georgia 73
Washington, George 60
Wayland, (Dr.) 21
Weelman, Jacob 12
Whit, (Mrs.) Polly 65
Whitaker, Grant 67
  Nancy 67
White, Bryant 12
  Richard 55
Wickson, Anna Maria 46
  Christina 46
  Jacob 46
Wilhelm (see Williams)
Willhelm (see Williams)
Williams, _____ 23, 62
  (Prof.) A. G. 37
  Floyd S. 62
  George 22, 37, 56, 60, 64
  Gertrude 72
  Henry 22
  John 62
  Margretha Harless 37
  Margarett 61
  Mary 55
  Michael 22
  Philip 22
Wilson, Mary 51
  Rachel 56
  Sam'l. K. 51
Wintrow, John 54, 63
  Mary 63
Wood, (Col.) Abraham 20
  (Gov.) James 58
  Richard 13
Wygall, (Miss) 74
  James 56
  Sebastian 56
Wyrick, (Rev.) H. P. 44

-Y-

Yonce, (Rev.) C. N. A. 43, 44

-Z-

Zanger (see also Stanger)
  Abraham 50
  Catherine 50
  Jacobus 50
  Ludwig 50
  Maria 50
  Peter 50
Zerfass (see Surface)
Zerwas (see Surface)
Zinglin, Peggy 65

www.ingramcontent.com/pod-product-compliance
Lightning Source LLC
Chambersburg PA
CBHW071226160426
43196CB00012B/2423